Little Labels—Big Sound

Gennett

5654-B

Fox Trot
12141
3-25

DAVENPORT BLUES
(Beiderbecke)

Bix & His Rhythm Jugglers

DIVISION OF
THE STARR PIANO CO.
RICHMOND
IND.

Little Labels—Big Sound

Small Record Companies and the Rise of American Music

Rick Kennedy and Randy McNutt

INDIANA UNIVERSITY PRESS BLOOMINGTON & INDIANAPOLIS

This book was published with
the kind support of
Pearl Shonfield.

Contents

FOREWORD

Passion.

That is the one common denominator in this book. While these are vignettes about the history of small independent labels, each label had a founder. Each founder had a motive in starting said label. Some did it for cash, some did it for love of music, and some did it because other people talked them into it. But once they got started, the passion came in and that is why we are reading about these labels/ gentlemen today.

I currently teach a course in Boston at The Berklee College of Music which is actually a history of record production. Many of these men are known to me and finally to my students, and I was fortunate enough to meet one or two of them in their lifetimes. They were all characters; that is, people with charisma of one sort or another.

There would be no record business as we know it without the passion of these pioneers. Today's leaders and label heads pale in comparison to these legendary giants. Show me a man today that could stand up to a Syd Nathan or a Don Robey, and I'll show you a man behind bars—not behind a desk. Why, without Sam Phillips, the founder of Sun Records and the man who unearthed Elvis, Carl Perkins, Johnny Cash, Roy Orbison, Jerry Lee Lewis, Rufus Thomas, and Howling Wolf to name but a few, there might not even have been any rock 'n' roll, electric blues, or rockabilly music.

And their passion has been passed on, especially to the authors of this fascinating book, Rick Kennedy and Randy McNutt. Their research seems exhaustive, thorough, and most importantly, non-revisionist. I feel I could pull any fact out of this book for any of my courses at school, and feel confident I was passing along the truth to a generation that needs to hear it. Above and beyond that, this book is fun to read. And why shouldn't it be? It's about some interesting, passionate men who enjoyed what they did for a living. And so shall you enjoy yourself as you settle down for a comfy read and an education at the same time. Is this a beautiful country or what???

Al Kooper
June 1998

PREFACE

From the 1920s through the 1960s, scores of small, independently owned record labels featured distinctly American music: jazz, blues, gospel, country, rhythm & blues (R&B), and its offspring, rock 'n' roll. Operated by individuals or families, these labels fostered America's musical voice over five decades with original music on the tide of social change and became influential and enduring. *Little Labels, Big Sound* celebrates 10 such labels.

Well-documented are the black and white musicians who attracted a world audience with American musical styles. However, we tend to forget the colorful owners of small labels who recognized the promise of many of these performers and helped to popularize a sound before larger, more bureaucratic record competitors knew what was happening. Many of these trailblazing labels crashed and burned as quickly as they rose.

Some small label owners were visionaries. Ross Russell, a record store owner in Los Angeles, California, in the mid-1940s, staked his last dollar to create Dial Records because he recognized that an obscure jazz saxophonist named Charlie Parker was creating a jazz revolution with bebop music. Because Sam Phillips, owner of Memphis Recording Service in Tennessee, had produced country and R&B singers, he knew what he had found after a shy, teenage Elvis Presley entered his storefront studio in 1953 and asked to make a personal recording. Later that decade, the three-octave voice of Roy Orbison, a struggling rockabilly singer/songwriter, astounded Fred Foster, who had just created Monument Records. Foster believed if he properly showcased Orbison, he would create a sensation.

Other owners didn't appreciate the music they recorded all that much, but they were street-smart entrepreneurs. White-owned "race" labels in the 1920s were indifferent to, or puzzled by, the blues singers they recorded, but the discs attracted black consumers. Many labels were extensions of a record store, booking agency, or nightclub. Don Robey named his influential R&B and gospel label "Peacock" after his 1940s nightclub in Houston, Texas, where he discovered promising acts. A former pawnshop operator, Syd Nathan sold used records to Appalachian and black customers in Cincinnati, Ohio, before he created King Records in 1943 and produced country and blues music.

Influencing music did not top the agenda of these visionaries and entrepreneurs; they first and foremost wanted to earn a living. Records happened to be less expensive to produce and distribute than other products, and they gave off the aura of show business. While major labels (typically, divisions of large manufacturers) were based almost exclusively in New York, Chicago, and Los Angeles, some independents managed to thrive in faraway cities like Houston, Memphis, Cincinnati, New Orleans, and Jackson, Mississippi. They promoted regional sounds and evolving musical styles that eventually reverberated around the world.

Nearly all independent labels created before 1970 have since closed or have been acquired by larger entertainment companies. Music company takeovers and the rise of international conglomerates in the past quarter-century make it nearly impossible for a tiny label to take a regional American music style and reach a broad audience. Small labels, however, continue to influence the musical landscape. In the 1990s, advances in digital sound technology have made home recording and compact disc (CD) replication more affordable for a plethora of small-time recording artists and labels catering to specialty audiences. In addition, small labels today are digitally remastering and reissuing on CD the influential music of long-gone labels, thus making previously out-of-print records available to new generations of listeners.

The abundance of early jazz, blues, gospel, R&B, country, and rock 'n' roll now available on reissue anthologies helped to inspire the writing of *Little Labels, Big Sound*. Our purpose was to profile record industry underdogs, who, despite tough odds, produced memorable music that is still very much with us. While these labels made lasting contributions, they were not selected for the book solely on their level of significance. If that were the case, Blue Note, Atlantic, Chess, Modern, and others would be profiled. (They are part of the book's opening chapter.) We selected 10 labels whose owners and musicians fascinated us, and we felt theirs were great stories of triumph deserving wider recognition. We concentrated on the early 1920s through the 1960s, during which time most American musical styles emerged. In addition, the passage of time allows the labels from that era to be placed in proper historical perspective.

Randy McNutt and I (Rick Kennedy) have long been fascinated by the commercial and social forces that impact the course of music. We first met in 1994 when Randy interviewed me for *The Cincinnati Enquirer* on my book about Gennett Records and the early jazz recording industry. Randy previously wrote a pictorial history of rockabilly music and produced pop, country, and rockabilly records. About an hour into our chat, this book collaboration became inevitable. Because we have experiences in different musical genres, we broadened the book's focus to include America's diverse musical styles. *Little Labels, Big Sound* was a blast to write as it took us on a marvelous journey. We hope our enthusiasm for these labels is catching.

The book came even more alive when people who owned these labels, or who were closely associated with them, provided us their recollections. They include the late Richard Gennett, John Steiner, Ross Russell, Zella Nathan, Orrin Keepnews, Fred Foster, Robert Koester, John Vincent, the late Henry Gennett Martin, Bud Dant, the late Marion McKay, Ryland Jones, Bruce Iglauer, the late Carl Perkins, Charlie Feathers, Barbara Pittman, Chuck Nessa, Wayne Moss, James Mattis, William Holford, Marcus Van Story, Hal Neely, the late Grandpa Jones, Malcolm Yelvington, Frankie Ford, and Roy Head.

Other special thanks also go to Dwight Weber and Jim Stump for their review of the manuscript; Jim Callaway for his photographic contributions; Robert Santelli at the Rock and Roll Hall of Fame and Museum; Gayle Dean Wardlow and Pete Whelan of 78 *Quarterly*; the International Association of Jazz Record Collectors; Gunnar Jacobson; Duncan Schiedt; David Oliphant; Eugene Miller; Nick Miller; Stan Kandebo; Guy Norris; Jim Mathews; Frank Powers; and Natalie Wrubel.

INTRODUCTION

Little Labels and the American Beat, 1920–1970

A select group of large music companies has always dominated the American record industry, which blossomed in the 1900s with three rival phonograph manufacturers: Victor, Columbia, and Edison. Using court rulings to their advantage, the three dominant companies squelched smaller competitors by protecting their numerous patents for phonograph and recording technology. In the century's opening years, Thomas Edison's original cylinder-playing machine, first introduced in 1877 as the "phonograph," gave way to a more practical, disc-playing machine, first called the "gramophone." By 1912, the popularity of Victor's and Columbia's 78-rpm shellac discs and gramophones, soon to be renamed "phonographs," forced Edison to manufacture both types of machines.

Around 1915, however, several phonograph manufacturing patents expired, and dozens of new phonograph manufacturers and record labels emerged. By then, Victor and Columbia commanded the phonograph and record market with discs by the leading symphony orchestras, opera stars, choral groups, brass bands, and stage singers who performed the era's popular sheet music. The first indigenous American music to be recorded was jazz. Conceived in the late 19th century by African-American and Creole musicians in New Orleans, jazz first gained national exposure through Victor's 1917 releases by the Original Dixieland Jazz Band, an accomplished white group whose lead instrumentalists grew up in New Orleans. The band sparked a national dance craze.

In the early 1920s, smaller record labels pursued rural and black urban audiences neglected by the major record companies. This increased competition was made possible as key recording-technology patents entered the public domain. The Starr Piano Company of Richmond, Indiana, owners of the Gennett label, opened this door by winning landmark patent cases in 1921–22 against Victor. In 1921, New York's OKeh label created a "race record" market with popular releases by Harlem blues singer Mamie Smith. In 1922, the obscure Sunshine label in Los Angeles recorded New Orleans trombonist Kid Ory, one of the first black jazz players from New Orleans to appear on a 78-rpm disc. In 1923–24, the Gennett label and the Paramount label, a division of the Wisconsin Chair Company, produced the first records by black New Orleans jazz pioneers based in Chicago: Jelly Roll Morton, Louis Armstrong, King Oliver, Freddie Keppard, and Johnny Dodds. Gennett and Paramount also ventured into black country blues, gospel, and white country (called "old time" or "hillbilly") music. In the mid-1920s, OKeh organized black studio bands in New York, led by Louis Armstrong, and produced landmark jazz records that would define the "hot jazz" era.

Later in the 1920s, several small labels sold discount records through mail-order catalogs, featuring black country blues and white hillbilly music from hundreds of obscure singers (generally accompanied with guitars and fiddles) who generally earned a pittance from the records. Vocal music on 78-rpms improved significantly on some labels with new electronic recording equipment introduced in 1925. OKeh's Fiddlin' John Carson, arguably country music's first recording star, attracted a large Southern following, while Paramount attracted black phonograph owners nationwide with dozens of recordings by Texas street singer Blind Lemon Jefferson.

During the decade, Victor and Columbia maintained a lock on the mainstream record market with classical and operatic music, vaudeville stars, pop crooner Rudy Vallee, and band leader Paul Whiteman, who commissioned George Gershwin's "Rhapsody in Blue" in 1924. Yet Victor and Columbia also followed the lead of the smaller labels and produced much of the decade's best jazz, blues, and country music, including such jazz artists as Armstrong, Fletcher Henderson, Duke Ellington, Bessie Smith, and Morton, and country singers Jimmie Rodgers and The Carter Family.

By the early 1930s, the combined impact of home radio and the Great Depression had decimated small labels. After Paramount, Gennett, Herwin, and others went bankrupt, many blues and country musicians never recorded again. In 1932, the record industry sold only six million records, one-sixth the volume sold in 1927. RCA's (Radio Corporation of America) acquisition of mighty Victor characterized the drastic changes underway as the radio became the nation's primary home entertainment. Live radio broadcasts and touring dance bands ushered in the swing era, led by clarinetist Benny Goodman, who recorded for RCA Victor. Late in the 1930s, record sales slowly recovered as labels benefited from improved sound technology. Leading radio performers, such as Bing Crosby, The Mills Brothers, The Ink Spots, and The Andrews Sisters, perfected the studio vocal performance with a new giant label, American Decca Records, a division of Decca Co. Ltd. of England. Decca made a huge impact on the American record scene by driving down the retail price of records.

The late 1930s produced rumblings of things to come. The American Record Corporation (ARC) recorded Mississippi Delta bluesman Robert Johnson in 1936 in a San Antonio, Texas, hotel room, and the next year in a Dallas, Texas, warehouse. While the sessions were inconsequential at the time, Johnson's recordings would loom large in the birth of rock music. In 1938, Milt Gabler created the Commodore label in his Manhattan jazz store and recorded saxophonists Coleman Hawkins and Lester Young, singer Billie Holiday, and numerous white traditional jazz players. Commodore helped to ignite a traditional jazz revival in New York in the 1940s. In 1939, Alfred Lion, an aficionado of boogie-woogie piano, formed Blue Note Records, a progressive label that remained at the jazz forefront for several decades. In addition, a new music publishing company, Broadcast Music Co., developed a huge catalog of country music songs that eventually found their way onto records.

The war years of the early 1940s further altered music trends.

Gasoline rationing, curfews, the draft, and the death of band leader Glenn Miller diminished the commercial clout of the touring big bands. Vocalists and sentimental songs marked the era, led by Frank Sinatra's prolific output on Columbia and bolstered by the increased popularity of the jukebox. In America's music center, Manhattan, jazz was turned upside down by the small-group bebop movement led by Charlie Parker, Thelonius Monk, and Dizzy Gillespie. While union recording bans limited bebop's early documentation, the music was first promoted by a growing number of tiny labels, including Dial, Manor, Clef, Meteor, and Savoy.

Black and white rural music re-emerged as a growing record industry segment in the 1940s. This revival coincided with the war-driven industrial boom and the migration of rural blacks and whites to well-paying factory jobs in America's urban centers. On Decca, saxophonist Louis Jordan popularized a blues-style dance music called rhythm and blues (R&B), and independent labels further developed the genre. On the West Coast, Modern, Specialty, Aladdin, and other labels recorded R&B along with traditional blues and jazz for black consumers. Other independents recording R&B in the 1940s included Don Robey's Peacock label in Houston, Texas, which also produced black gospel, and Syd Nathan's King Records in Cincinnati, Ohio, though King was initially a "hillbilly label."

Developments in sound technology contributed to a proliferation of independent labels in the late 1940s and early 1950s. Responding to Columbia's 1948 introduction of the long-playing, 33-rpm album, RCA Victor introduced 45-rpm "singles" in 1949, which soon blared from cheap, portable record players. The 1940s arrival of magnetic tape recording technology eliminated the need to record a live or studio performance directly onto a blank disc. It created more flexibility in studio production by allowing "overdubbing" of taped performances. These changes made the recording business more attractive to small-time operators anxious to exploit an expanding economy and rapidly growing record segment among young people. From 1948 to 1954, about 1,000 new record labels were formed. By the early 1950s, the 45-rpm single format overtook the venerable 78-

rpm disc, though the latter was popular several more years with country and R&B record buyers.

The 1950s decade was the golden era for small independents, which embraced blues, gospel, modern jazz, country, R&B, and rock 'n' roll. In 1951, *Billboard* changed its "race chart" for black music to the "R&B chart," a recognition of black music's broader appeal. The mainstream record industry had long based its success on the American popular song, personified by such composers as Irving Berlin, George Gershwin, Hoagy Carmichael, Jerome Kern, Cole Porter, and Richard Rodgers. In the early 1950s, popular music collided with a new breed of country, blues, and R&B performers, many of whom combined singing and songwriting on a plethora of small labels such as Chess, Atlantic, Sun, King, Duke, Peacock, Specialty, Bullet, Imperial, Prestige, Cobra, Keen, Del-Fi, and Trumpet. For many small-budget independents, it came down to what music could be recorded most cheaply.

Among the most successful of these new independents was Atlantic, a New York label created in 1949 by Ahmet Ergeun and Herb Abramson to promote black music. Atlantic singing star Clyde McPhatter (eventually lead voice for the Drifters) attracted a large R&B following. By 1954, behind studio producer Jerry Wexler, Atlantic had released refined, pop-oriented sounds by such black vocal groups as the Chords, who recorded the popular "Sh-Boom." Other Atlantic artists included Joe Turner, Ruth Brown, and Ray Charles, who produced a string of gospel-inspired R&B hits in the mid-1950s.

In 1950, two immigrant brothers, Leonard and Phil Chess, created the Chess label and produced traditional blues with electric guitars. Chess-produced R&B, as sung by Chuck Berry, helped to define rock 'n' roll. The brothers had moved to Chicago in 1928, sold liquor after Prohibition was repealed, and eventually operated bars on the city's predominantly black South Side. They bought into the Aristocrat label in 1947 and signed local acts. Within a year, they recorded Muddy Waters, the Delta blues singer/guitarist and a leading black entertainer in Chicago. Assuming full ownership of Aristocrat in 1950, the Chess brothers changed the label to Chess and formed a subsidiary label, Checker. Over the next several years, Chess produced some of the greatest blues records ever with Waters, Elmore James, Howlin' Wolf, Little Walter, Sonny Boy Williamson, and Willie Dixon, the label's house composer and arranger who wrote "Hoochie Coochie Man," "Little Red Rooster," and other future rock standards.

In the mid-1950s, independents drove the commercial evolution of R&B into rock 'n' roll. Bill Haley, who recorded the smash hit "Rock Around the Clock" on Decca in 1954, had earlier gained popularity as a hillbilly and R&B singer on the tiny Essex label. In 1955, Berry, an R&B singer/guitarist with a country feel, debuted on Chess with a string of classics, while another rock pioneer, Bo Diddley, debuted on Checker. Little Richard, after struggling for years as a gospel and R&B singer, hit in the mid-1950s on Art Rupe's Specialty label in Hollywood and raised the voltage of rock 'n' roll with "Tutti Frutti" and other future rock standards. Several independents converged on New Orleans, where R&B pianist Fats Domino became a national sensation for Imperial. King Records turned primarily to R&B by the mid-1950s, and produced Bill Doggett, Earl Bostic, and James Brown.

However, no one compared to Elvis Presley in thrusting rock 'n' roll into the mainstream culture. By blending R&B, gospel, and country with his own singing style, Presley was the biggest act to rise from a small independent. He first gained regional notice in 1954–55 on Sam Phillips' Sun label in Memphis. Earlier, Phillips had produced blues and R&B for Chess and Modern with B. B. King, Ike Turner, Howlin' Wolf, and others. In 1952, he created Sun, a catalyst for the influential R&B and country hybrid called "rockabilly." In late 1955, Phillips sold Presley's contract to RCA, where the singer reached an international audience with "Heartbreak Hotel" and "Hound Dog," first recorded years before by Big Mama Thornton on Peacock. After Presley joined RCA, the Sun label continued to shape rock 'n' roll with Southern rockabilly singers Carl Perkins ("Blue Suede Shoes"), Jerry Lee Lewis ("Great Balls of Fire"), Johnny Cash, Roy Orbison, and Charlie Rich.

The rock 'n' roll phenomenon catapulted record sales from $213 million in 1954 to more than $450 million in 1957. During this time, rock 'n' roll also reached a wider audience through what was known as the "white cover," whereby white singers produced softer renditions of black R&B songs. Many small music companies held the copyrights to songs written by their R&B performers, so they readily offered material to established white singers, such as crooner Pat Boone, who rivaled Presley in record sales in the late 1950s.

Country music, once maligned as "hillbilly" music, became more pop-oriented in the 1950s through the major labels Decca, RCA, Capitol, MGM, and Mercury. These labels established offices and recording studios in Nashville and produced performers from the Grand Ole Opry stage. Guitarist Chet Atkins managed RCA's Nashville studio and eventually supervised all of RCA's operations in the city. Atkins' use of strings and smooth vocal harmonies influenced country music production for many years.

Small independents, however, provided exposure to country giants who later became mainstays on the major labels. Among the first and most important was Hank Williams, who debuted in 1946 on Sterling, a small New York label, before jumping to MGM. In 1954, a year after Williams' death, George Jones debuted on his manager's small label, Starday, before moving on to major record companies. Around that time, Patsy Cline debuted on the Four Star label in California, before joining Decca. Bill Anderson recorded and wrote songs for the Tanner 'N' Texas label (TNT) in San Antonio before joining Decca. A singer/housewife named Loretta Lynn went door-to-door to country radio stations with her first record, "I'm a Honky Tonk Girl," on the little-known Zero label. The early 1960s folk revival was fostered by Moe Asch's Folkways label, formed in 1956, which released influential albums by singers and string players Doc Watson, Woody Guthrie, and Pete Seeger.

In the 1950s, independent labels supported the development of modern jazz, which was freed from the time restrictions of the 78-rpm disc by the 33-rpm long-playing album format. In Los Angeles, Lester Koenig's Contemporary and Richard Bock's Pacific Jazz promoted "cool" jazz with saxophonists Art Pepper and Gerry Mulligan, drummer Shelly Manne, and trumpeter Chet Baker. On the East Coast, Bob Weinstock's Prestige recorded saxophonist Sonny Rollins and trumpeter Miles Davis, while Orrin Keepnews' Riverside produced pianists Thelonius Monk and Bill Evans and guitarist Wes Montgomery. Vanguard, under the direction of John Hammond, produced swing jazz by Buck Clayton, Count Basie, and others. Blue Note gave jazz a harder and more soulful edge with trumpeters Freddie Hubbard and Lee Morgan, saxophonists Jackie McLean and Wayne Shorter, organist Jimmy Smith, and pianist Horace Silver. Atlantic recorded saxophonists John Coltrane and Ornette Coleman and bassist Charles Mingus. Atlantic preceded the influential Impulse! label, a subsidiary of ABC-Paramount, in promoting the emerging free jazz movement. Veteran jazz promoter Norman Granz, founder of the Clef and Norgran labels, formed the Verve label in 1956 in Los Angeles and produced memorable records by singer Ella Fitzgerald in refined, orchestral settings. In 1960, MGM acquired Verve and produced jazz innovators Bill Evans, Stan Getz, and Wes Montgomery in a pop-oriented vein.

As in previous decades, the major labels in the 1950s promoted established jazz acts with broader commercial appeal, such as Duke Ellington, Stan Kenton, Woody Herman, and Louis Armstrong. Columbia, arguably the most inventive of the major labels recording jazz, signed Miles Davis in the mid-1950s and produced landmark albums, including collaborations with arranger Gil Evans and the small-group classic "Kind of Blue." The Dave Brubeck Quartet obtained huge commercial success with the Columbia album "Time Out."

Record industry consolidation, the rise of music and entertainment conglomerates, and rock music as big business characterized the 1960s. By 1964, the Beatles, from Liverpool, England, had taken rock music to new commercial heights by attracting both teenagers and young adults. The American pop music scene had never faced such a formidable "foreign" presence. Taking note of the Beatles' success in America, the major labels aggressively promoted rock performers and gradually dominated the songs on the youth-oriented radio stations. (By the early 1960s, Columbia, a rock hold-out, signed Bob Dylan and the U.S. rock band, Paul Revere and the Raiders.)

First inspired by 1950s R&B and rockabilly on America's independent labels, the Beatles initially failed to reach American audiences in 1963 on the small Tollie, Swan, and Vee Jay labels. By the following year, they ruled the American charts after signing with British EMI Records' American subsidiary, Capitol Records. The Beatles fueled a British pop and rock invasion into the United States that forced the early rock pioneers to scramble for work and record contracts. From 1965 through 1967, the Beatles and their American rivals on Capitol, the Beach Boys, popularized album-oriented rock, characterized by elaborate studio production and editing. Competing on this more expensive level became a risky proposition for small labels facing inferior distribution capability and limited radio airplay. The rock industry had grown up and joined the music establishment, and small family-owned independents felt the squeeze.

While country blues experienced a brief revival in the early 1960s, jazz recordings faced a commercial drought that lasted almost 20 years. Even Count Basie and Louis Armstrong consented to record 1960s pop and rock hits. A painful example was Armstrong's recording of John Lennon's "Give Peace a Chance." Still, the 1960s produced memorable jazz for a smaller audience, such as the radical work of saxophonist John Coltrane and pianist Cecil Taylor on the Impulse! label. In addition, Blue Note's funk-oriented musicians, including pianist Herbie Hancock, made commercial inroads. Small independents, such as the Delmark and Nessa labels, which captured Chicago's free jazz movement, continued to support jazz, although most operated on a shoestring. One of jazz's few commercial superstars with young audiences in the 1960s, Miles Davis ushered in the era of fusion, a blend of jazz and rock on electrical instruments, with a series of influential records on Columbia.

Some 1960s independent labels still managed to shape American music and reach the pop charts, particularly with white country and black music. Fred Foster's Monument label in Nashville created a pop sensation with Roy Orbison, discovered Dolly Parton, and later made songwriter-cum-singer Kris Kristofferson a household name. Black R&B evolved into the youthful sound of soul music behind innovative releases from Chicago's Chess and Vee Jay labels, Cincinnati's King label (with James Brown), Berry Gordy's Motown hit factory in Detroit, and Jim Stewart's Stax, a Southern soul label based in Memphis. While attracting a huge white and black audience to classic 1960s soul music, these independents ultimately fell into the hands of larger corporations.

Since the 1970s, small independents have continued to influence American music by focusing more on target audiences. The many examples include Bruce Iglauer's Chicago-based Alligator Records, which sparked a 1980s blues revival, and Manfred Eicher's ECM label in Germany, which attracted a world audience to the ethereal jazz of Americans Keith Jarrett, Gary Burton, and Pat Metheny. Protesting the corporate packaging of rock music, dozens of tiny U.S. and British labels advanced the cause of non-commercial punk rock, "go-go," and rap music in the late 1970s and 1980s.

In recent years, more affordable digital sound technology has created a new era for small independents. While receiving little or no commercial radio airplay, thousands of homegrown labels reach niche audiences by efficiently packaging and marketing CDs. The Internet and desktop publishing provide these labels with market access unimagined a few years ago. As in the past, these labels provide a springboard for music styles soon adopted by major music companies. For example, before "alternative rock" became a huge music industry segment in the 1990s, Seattle-based "grunge" rock was embraced by tiny labels. In 1988, for example, the label Sub Pop debuted Nirvana, a bellwether "alternative rock band." Reacting to highly produced, mainstream country music of the 1990s, several tiny labels are promoting a more grassroots, homespun country genre now called "Americana."

While most small record labels operate in obscurity, history will ultimately side with those producing memorable music. Nobody in the early 1920s anticipated the impact the Gennett and Paramount labels would have on jazz. In the 1930s, who could have imagined that bluesman Robert Johnson's obscure ARC recording sessions would sell on CD by the tens of thousands each year in the 1990s? The record industry titans in the early 1950s ignored Sun Records until Elvis Presley created hysteria across the South, and Sun Records is now part of music folklore. Without question, little-known labels today are producing original American artists who will influence and amaze future generations of listeners.

Little Labels—Big Sound

One / **Gennett Records**

"The studio was a dreary looking Rube Goldberg place with lily-shaped horns sticking oddly from the walls. It didn't have the effect of soothing me."

—Hoagy Carmichael, composer of "Stardust"

In April 1923, King Oliver's Creole Jazz Band, the rage of Chicago's black nightclub district, took a five-hour train ride across rural Indiana to the Starr Piano factory in the small industrial town of Richmond. The sprawling factory complex, operated by Henry Gennett and his three sons, sat secluded beside a river in a vast glacial gorge known locally as Starr Valley. The family also produced its own Gennett record label in a primitive, wood-framed studio along the factory's railway line. Musicians crowded around megaphone-style horns, as a recording stylus etched sound vibrations directly onto blank, soft-wax discs.

Though wildly popular at Chicago's Lincoln Gardens dance hall, cornetist Oliver and his young New Orleans jazz players had never stepped into a recording studio. "It was something none of us had experienced and we were all very nervous," drummer Baby Dodds said. "We were all working hard and perspiration as big as a thumb dropped off us."[1] The studio engineer recorded 28 takes in the hot, non-ventilated room. Oliver's second cornetist, future legend Louis Armstrong, stood farthest from the acoustic horns for fear that his Herculean tone would cause the needle to bounce on the wax master disc. Oliver's group caught the next available train back to Chicago. The Gennett studio staff carefully packed the fragile wax discs from the session and delivered them to the factory's metal-plating room for processing, unaware of the history they had just preserved.

The first batch of Oliver's 78-rpm shellac discs released on Gennett captured a landmark day in American music, and the most significant jazz recording session to that point. Although the first jazz records were produced in New York in 1917 by the Original Dixieland Jazz Band, the Oliver sides from April 1923 in Richmond are considered jazz music's first recorded masterpieces. These old Gennett discs document a highly refined, polyphonic New Orleans ensemble tradition, brilliant solos by Armstrong, Oliver, and clarinetist Johnny Dodds, and several original compositions from the seminal group of early 1920s jazz.

It would seem to be a remarkable coup for a small record company in rural Indiana, more than 60 miles from the closest major

Little Labels—Big Sound

cities of Indianapolis, Indiana, and Cincinnati, Ohio. Yet, in fact, Gennett Records, by documenting the convergence of New Orleans and Midwestern jazz musicians in early 1920s Chicago, debuted a remarkable parade of future jazz giants: Oliver, Armstrong, Jelly Roll Morton, Bix Beiderbecke, Leon Roppolo, George Brunies, Freddie Keppard, and Earl "Fatha" Hines. Gennett's association with Chicago jazz led Indiana composer Hoagy Carmichael to Richmond, where he recorded his first songs, including the timeless "Stardust."

The Gennetts sold records to black and rural people largely neglected by the dominant New York labels. In addition to Gennett, the family produced a discount label, Champion, and also recorded and pressed discs for Sears' mail-order discount labels, targeted for rural buyers in the 1920s. This market focus encouraged the Richmond studio not only to pioneer jazz recording, but also to produce some of the first discs by country blues singers, Appalachian string bands and white country gospel groups—traditional regional music that was the bedrock of country-western and early rock 'n' roll. Gennett's notable country and blues singers included Gene Autry, Vernon Dalhart, Bill Broonzy, Bradley Kincaid, Ernest Stoneman, and Roosevelt Sykes. Before collapsing during the 1930s Great Depression, Gennett Records preserved and promoted the soulful, undiluted sounds of America's musical grassroots.

The legacy was unintentional. The Gennetts were not musical visionaries, but hard-nosed piano manufacturers and retailers who sold records as a sideline business. Starr Piano, founded in 1872, first blossomed along Richmond's Whitewater River in the late 19th century under owners James and Benjamin Starr. In 1893, Henry Gennett, a slight, swarthy Italian from Nashville, Tennessee, bought into the company and moved his family to Richmond. Within a decade, he and his three sons, Clarence, Harry, and Fred, acquired control of Starr Piano, which they developed into one of the nation's largest piano manufacturers. By 1915, Starr Piano produced 15,000 pianos annually, selling them through a chain of stores in Ohio and Indiana, and in the cities of New York, Detroit, San Diego, and Los Angeles.

In quaint Richmond, Indiana, a prosperous town of 25,000

3

people, the Gennetts were quintessential small-town business leaders in America's Victorian Age. Henry, often sporting a white Panama hat and cane with a gold knob, and his impeccably dressed wife, Alice, daughter of a Nashville millionaire, supported the local symphony, financed visits from touring performers, and created a 1,200-seat Gennett Theater downtown. They built a mansion on Richmond's Main Street with a spacious third-floor ballroom. Their three sons each raised families in stately homes a short walk from their parents and a few blocks from their piano factory, the town's industrial cornerstone.

With piano sales booming, the Gennetts expanded in 1915 into phonographs and records, a sporty new industry dominated by New Jersey's Victor Talking Machine Co. Starr Piano built recording studios above its Manhattan store and in Richmond's Starr Valley. But sales for Starr records lagged because independent dealers avoided selling records so closely associated with Starr pianos. Even worse, vertical-cut Starr records, like Edison's Diamond discs, couldn't be played on the ubiquitous Victor and Columbia phonographs, which played only lateral-cut records.

The Gennetts changed the label's name to "Gennett" to minimize the Starr association. Then, in 1919, they challenged Victor by introducing their own lateral-cut records, a technology protected by Victor patents. Victor sued Starr Piano for patent infringement, and several court battles ensued, with Starr supported by other small record companies. Ultimately, the courts ruled that Victor did not invent lateral-cut recording technology. Starr Piano's final court victory in 1922 put the technology into the public domain, thus allowing smaller labels to compete in an industry virtually controlled by the giants Victor, Columbia, and Edison.

The early 1920s, before the dawn of cheap home radios, were peak years for Gennett Records. While still dwarfed by New York's leading labels, the Richmond pressing plant pressed millions of eclectic discs: symphonies, opera and black-faced vaudeville singers, ethnic language, comedy dialogue, exercise records, sacred choirs and soloists, speeches and prayers by William Jennings Bryan, ma-

4

rimba bands, marching brass bands, xylophone trios, and hotel dance orchestras.

Gennett also custom-pressed thousands of discs for the Ku Klux Klan. These discs were often adaptations of sacred hymns, such as "The Bright Fiery Cross" (based on "The Old Rugged Cross"), "Onward Christian Klansmen" ("Onward Christian Soldiers"), and "Cross by the Wildwood" ("Church by the Wildwood"). While many Starr Piano employees were active in the local klavern, the Gennetts didn't participate. They quietly pressed the discs because the Klan paid cash for all the discs pressed.

In mid-1922, Gennett Records made its historic venture into Chicago jazz. Prohibition-era Chicago, with the nation's largest black urban population, was a lightning rod for black and white New Orleans jazz players, who attracted large crowds in the city's numerous dance halls and speakeasies. Fred Wiggins, manager of Starr Piano's downtown Chicago store, was taken by a young, white jazz band at the nearby, mob-controlled Friars Inn. He urged his boss and longtime friend, Fred Gennett, to set up a recording date in Richmond for the band, known as the New Orleans Rhythm Kings (NORK).

Fred Gennett, a small, thin man of 36 with receding black hair and horn-rimmed glasses, headed the record division. He lacked his father's hard-edged business skills. "Pop was a smart fella, but money never meant anything to him," recalled Fred's son, Richard. [2] Fred had no personal interest in jazz, but to his brothers' chagrin, he was attracted to the latest fads. "It drove the family at Starr Piano half-crazy, but if it was something new, Pop would try it," his son added.

Fred Gennett also had confidence in Fred Wiggins, a thin man with a high-pitched voice and a stogie perpetually dangling from his mouth. Wiggins was born in Richmond and joined Starr Piano in the shipping department in 1906. He rose through the sales department to become manager of Starr's Chicago store. Notoriously opinionated, Wiggins, who was 46 years old in 1922, had no training in music but kept close tabs on Chicago's young musicians, looking for business opportunities.

5

Fred Gennett, shown here holding his sons, was the innovative manager of the Gennett Records division of the Starr Piano Company in Richmond, Indiana. Despite his lack of interest in jazz, he released the music's first recorded masterpieces.

Since 1919, the Gennett label had recorded numerous jazz-style, commercial bands in its Manhattan studio. But with Chicago's more distinct sound of pure New Orleans jazz still untapped by the large record companies, Fred Gennett heeded Wiggins' advice and signed the eight-piece NORK, fronted by three New Orleans players: trombonist George Brunies, cornetist Paul Mares, and the remarkable Leon Roppolo on clarinet. In August 1922, the musicians loaded a sedan, strapped their instruments to the running boards, and headed to the Richmond studio for the first of three recording sessions with Gennett.

They found the studio in a gray wooden warehouse, along a row of factory buildings. It stood three feet from a secondary railroad spur for slow-moving cars hauling freight through the congested factory.

Little Labels — Big Sound

To make matters worse, the main Chesapeake & Ohio railroad ran above the Starr Piano factory along the ridge of Starr Valley, also producing tremendous noise and vibration. Because of the two railroad lines, recording sessions were frequently interrupted. The studio's attempt at soundproofing involved packing sawdust between the studio's interior and exterior walls. Inside, sound resonance was minimized by hanging monk's cloth draperies from ceiling to floor. A large Mohawk rug from Harry Gennett's home was hung on one wall.

Situated in a humid river gorge, the studio was naturally hot in the summer. But to keep the blank wax master discs soft for recording, the studio was kept hot year-round. Achieving proper sound balance, which could take hours, required placing performers at various distances from the recording horns. Numerous wax test records were made and played back through the horns. Certain musicians, such as banjo players, were positioned on high stools. Brass players stood farthest from the horns.

The Gennetts rarely hired music professionals for the Richmond studio and generally recruited staff from the piano factory. This practice proved significant, especially for jazz, blues, and country musicians visiting the studio, because the staff simply waxed the discs and didn't intrude. Not only were musicians free to express themselves, but the staff allowed them to record their own songs. With music publishing still dominant over the emerging record industry, studios commonly required musicians to play only the popular published tunes. The Gennett studio offered more latitude and thus provided an atmosphere for greater creativity.

This freedom clearly benefited the NORK. Of the band's 31 sides issued on Gennett in 1922–23, several original songs, including "Tin Roof Blues," "Bugle Call Blues," and "Farewell Blues," became standards in the early jazz repertoire. Equally significant, these records preserved the fluid, emotional improvisations by clarinetist Roppolo, an eccentric Sicilian who was arguably the first jazz virtuoso ever recorded. (Within a few years, Roppolo would begin a lifetime confinement in a mental institution.) Gennett's NORK releases caused a sensation with aspiring musicians in 1920s Chi-

7

cago, including future jazz stars Bud Freeman and Jimmy Mc-
Partland.

Brisk sales for the NORK releases led Gennett to Chicago's
most celebrated black jazz band, King Oliver's Creole Jazz Band.
Among the 13 songs released from two visits to Richmond in 1923,
the Oliver band debuted several future jazz classics, such as "Dipper-
mouth Blues," by Oliver and Armstrong; "Chimes Blues," "Just
Gone," and "Snake Rag," each by Oliver; and "Weather Bird Rag," by
Armstrong. All were highly original numbers created for the Gennett
sessions. Through its "Gennett Colored Artists" catalog, Gennett
sold the Oliver releases with several white jazz bands, including the
NORK.

Gennett's Oliver releases helped preserve a brief, memorable
period in history when Armstrong teamed with Oliver, his only
acknowledged musical mentor. They created breathtaking, tele-
pathic cornet duets, the likes of which the world of jazz has rarely
heard since. Within a year of its first session on Gennett, the legendary Oliver band dissolved. Louis and Lillian Armstrong and Johnny
Dodds made history in 1925–26 with their Hot Five recordings on
OKeh Records. By the late 1930s, Oliver had faded into obscurity
and died a penniless janitor, while Armstrong was an international
star.

Original compositions on Gennett by the NORK and Oliver
bands were sold as stock arrangements and sheet music by small-time
Chicago music publishers Walter and Lester Melrose. Combined,
Gennett discs and Melrose Brothers sheet music made Chicago jazz
accessible to a national audience. Certain Melrose stock arrangements often referenced the corresponding Gennett discs to provide
further musical guidance. Equally important, the Gennett-Melrose
connection led Fred Gennett to preserve the timeless artistry of
pianist Jelly Roll Morton, a Melrose staff composer and self-pro-
claimed inventor of jazz.

The well-traveled Morton, another New Orleans musician
seeking his fortune in Chicago, had been a pool hustler, pimp, club
operator, vaudeville performer, ragtime piano virtuoso, and published composer when he visited Richmond in mid-1923. At the

8

Jazz icon Louis Armstrong debuted on record with the Gennett and Paramount labels in 1923 as a cornetist with King Oliver's Creole Jazz Band. Within a decade, he was internationally renowned.

session, Morton teamed with the NORK on what is considered the first interracial recording session in jazz history. (The NORK secured Morton a hotel room in Richmond by claiming he was Latin American, according to the NORK's Brunies.) Gennett released six sides

9

from the collaboration, including versions of Morton classics "Mr. Jelly Lord" and "Milenberg Joys." His ragtime-style piano lends a pleasant, easy-going atmosphere to these records while his songs were an excellent vehicle for Roppolo's lyrical improvisations.

During 1923–24, Gennett also released 15 sides of Morton on solo piano. These low-fidelity recordings are noted for Morton's lightning piano runs, intricate counterpoint, and for the multi-thematic nature of his compositions, such as "Wolverine Blues," "The Pearls," and "King Porter Stomp." These solo performances, which become more celebrated with each passing year, comprise one of only three series of recordings produced by Morton during his lifetime. The 1923 collaboration with Morton was the NORK's last Gennett session. Within two years, the group disbanded after Chicago's Friars Inn opted for a new floor show. Yet, during the band's reign there, the Friars Inn attracted scores of young jazz musicians.

Several of them became Gennett artists. On a college break in the early 1920s, Hoagy Carmichael, an Indiana University (IU) law student, piano player, and jazz fanatic, journeyed to the Friars Inn, where, at one of the small cabaret tables, he first met Bix Beiderbecke, an amazing white cornetist from Iowa. Their paths crossed again in 1924 when Beiderbecke headed the Wolverine Orchestra, a fledgling jazz band that barnstormed Ohio and Indiana, lived hand-to-mouth, and recorded for Gennett. Carmichael booked the band for Greek parties at IU in Bloomington, Indiana. Carmichael, who led his own campus jazz band, was mesmerized by Beiderbecke's gorgeous tone and improvisations. Their eccentric personalities, and mutual interests in music and bootleg whiskey suited each other. They fast became close friends. On a drunken Sunday at IU's Kappa Sigma house, Beiderbecke encouraged Carmichael to pursue his desire to compose music. Some weeks later, Carmichael assembled the Wolverines around a piano to debut his first song. To Carmichael's astonishment, the Wolverines recorded the untried New Orleans–style song, ultimately called "Riverboat Shuffle," in Richmond in May 1924. Carmichael received a contract from New York's Irving Mills for the song's publishing rights and a remarkable composing career was underway.

10

Little Labels—Big Sound

Over the next several months, the Wolverines found work in Indiana and finally at New York's Cinderella Ballroom. Gennett issued more than a dozen Wolverines sides, providing an aural diary of Beiderbecke's early musical development. When he joined the more-established Jean Goldkette Orchestra in October 1924, the Wolverines were doomed.

Perhaps Beiderbecke's greatest triumph on Gennett was his last Richmond recording session in January 1925, when he was out of work and drifting around the Midwest. Carmichael drove him to Richmond to meet friends from Goldkette's band, most notably trombonist Tommy Dorsey, who arrived with bottles of gin. With little written down, the six-piece pickup band produced an arrangement for a melody Beiderbecke created, which he dubbed "Davenport Blues." The record, issued under Bix and His Rhythm Jugglers, preserved his advanced explorations into rhythm and harmony. Six years later, Beiderbecke died from dissipation at age 28.

Carmichael's association with Gennett, on the other hand, had just begun. In early 1925, a jazz band from southern Indiana, Curtis Hitch's Happy Harmonists, recorded Carmichael's "Washboard Blues" in Richmond with the composer on piano. "The studio was a dreary looking Rube Goldberg place with lily-shaped horns sticking oddly from the walls," Carmichael later wrote. "It didn't have the effect of soothing me. The horns sticking from the walls looked spooky and I was pretty upset by the time we were ready to make test records." [3] When the first test record of "Washboard Blues" came up 20 seconds short, Carmichael filled out the recording with an impromptu piano solo. (Years later, that solo became the framework for Carmichael's 1933 hit "Lazybones.")

After completing law school in 1926, Carmichael pursued the uncertain career path of jazz musician and composer. In 1927, while based in central Indiana, he experimented with a melody he said was inspired by a lost romance from his IU days. He arranged the song in ragtime style and played it at local gigs. An IU student dubbed the song "Star Dust," the title to be changed ultimately to "Stardust."

In October 1927, Carmichael recruited Indianapolis band leader Emil Seidel, and seven members of his band, and drove

11

through the night across Indiana to the Richmond piano factory to debut "Star Dust" on record. Carmichael got Gennett recording engineer Harold Soule out of bed at 3 A.M. "I got the first take at 5 o'clock in the morning," Soule recalled. "Old Hoagy fell backwards off his piano stool and says, 'My masterpiece,' and it was." [4] The ragged, up-tempo instrumental rendition of "Star Dust" on Gennett is a remarkable glimpse into the birth of an American classic. The record's highlight is Carmichael's meandering, contrapuntal piano solo. Haunted by the song's melody, reminiscent of a Beiderbecke improvisation, Carmichael later recalled: "Back there in the old ratty recording studio, I was vague in mood as the strains hung in the rafters of the place. I wanted to shout, 'Maybe I didn't write you, but I found you.'" [5]

Gennett paid Carmichael the standard one penny per side in royalties. Musicians never got rich off Gennett royalties, and Carmichael's "Star Dust" earnings probably only covered expenses to travel to Richmond and back. Undaunted, he returned the following spring with another pickup band of Indiana players. "We never really thought much about cutting a record," said Bud Dant, then an IU freshman and the session's cornetist. "Jazz was so new in those days and we just thought going over to Richmond with Hoagy would be a kick." [6] Gennett issued two excellent sides from the session, Carmichael's "March of the Hoodlums" and a standard, "Walkin' the Dog," with Carmichael on scat vocal and playing unsteady cornet.

At the session, Carmichael made a second recording of "Star Dust," on which he sang his own lyrics. Fred Wiggins, who was now the Richmond studio supervisor for Fred Gennett, reviewed the "Star Dust" take and wrote on the recording information card: "Reject. Already on Gennett. Poor seller." By 1930, Carmichael had moved to New York where Mitchell Parish added lyrics to "Stardust," now a one-word title. Within a few years, Carmichael was a major composer on Tin Pan Alley and "Stardust" was America's most recorded song.

Carmichael's rise in the music industry coincided with the steady decline of Gennett's recording division. It stayed in operation, in large part, due to Fred Gennett's resourcefulness. From 1925 to

Hoagy Carmichael, law graduate of Indiana University and confidant of trumpeter Bix Beiderbecke, debuted his future classic "Star Dust" on Gennett Records in 1927. It barely sold.

Gennett Records

1928, the Richmond studio recorded hundreds of sides and pressed millions of discs for Sears' mail-order record labels, such as Silvertone and Challenge. Also, Gennett's Champion label (sold at three records for $1) duplicated the Gennett master discs with the artists' true identities hidden behind pseudonyms.

Many Gennett artists knew nothing of this practice and never received the tiny royalties owed them for the Champion releases. In naming artists for the Champion label, the Richmond staff commonly paged through the telephone book or used names of friends and relatives. Some pseudonyms were downright ridiculous; the Fletcher Henderson orchestra on Gennett became Jack's Fast Steppin' Bell Hops on Champion, while Syd Valentine & His Patent Leather Kids became Skillet Dick & His Frying Pans.

In the latter half of the 1920s, sales diminished even further for the mainstay "Electrobeam Gennett" label, the name given the label with the advent of electronic recording. No longer at the jazz forefront, the Richmond studio turned to country music (called "old time" or "hillbilly" music), and, to a lesser extent, country blues. "All the Gennetts were interested in was hillbilly music," said Joe Geier, a Gennett studio engineer in the late 1920s. "That's where they made their money, because the Gennetts catered to Sears, and Sears catered to the hillbillies." [7]

Dennis Taylor, a Kentucky farmer, recruited more than a hundred Appalachian musicians, most notably Fiddlin' Doc Roberts, for sessions in Richmond, where the discs were pressed on the Gennett, Champion, and Sears labels. Gennett paid royalties to Taylor, who paid the naive rural musicians a few dollars for each recording date. For a short time, Gennett set up a studio in Chicago and recorded country singers from the Sears-owned WLS (World's Largest Store) radio station, such as Bradley Kincaid (one of America's first national radio singing stars) and Chubby Parker. Reminiscent of the Richmond studio, Gennett's Chicago studio on South Wabash Avenue was frequently interrupted by noise from a nearby elevated passenger railway.

In late 1926, Fred Gennett recorded Native Americans. He and an Arizona resort operator conjured up the idea of recording Hopi

Before becoming a singing cowboy matinee idol, Gene Autry was a Gennett "hillbilly" artist in the late 1920s and early 1930s, when the struggling label focused on rural customers.

15

Gennett Records

Indian tribes and selling the discs to Grand Canyon tourists. The Gennetts took a portable recording truck to Arizona and produced several sides. These were probably the first purely ethnic discs ever issued by a commercial record label. But Hopi songs such as "Tacheuktu Katcina" never reached the Hit Parade.

To compete in the race market, Gennett recorded black blues and gospel singers at the Richmond and New York studios and at temporary studios in Chicago and in Birmingham, Alabama. Between 1927 and 1934, Gennett's blues lineup included Cow Cow Davenport, Thomas Dorsey, Cryin' Sam Collins, William Harris, Bill Broonzy, Jelly Roll Anderson, Lottie Kimbrough (dubbed the "Kansas City Butterball"), Willie Baker, and Mae Glover. As with the "hillbilly" discs, Gennett issued the same blues performance on the Gennett, Champion, and Sears labels.

Gennett was notorious for low overhead. Blues singers were paid $5 to $15 per recording session with no royalties. As for lodging in Richmond, they relied on boarding houses in a black neighborhood known as "Goose Town," a sort of red-light, speakeasy district north of the downtown railroad tracks. If musicians missed recording dates, there was a good chance they were hanging out in Goose Town. In such cases, Gennett called on Starr employee Charlie Yeager. "Yeager knew every house in the north end that sold bootleg whiskey, mountain dew, or what," said Clayton Jackson, a Gennett staffer. "He knew where to look for them [musicians]. He could go there after these people without any trouble. If anybody else went down there, it was pretty dangerous." [8]

During mid-1927, Gennett created a portable studio in its Starr Piano store in Birmingham to record a variety of black culture, from Baptist minister Reverend J. F. Forrest, with his rousing sermon "Hell and What It Is," to William Harris, possibly the first Mississippi Delta blues player ever recorded. Alabama blues harmonica player Jaybird Coleman recorded several sides, including the cerebral "Ah'm Sick and Tired of Tellin' You (To Wiggle That Thing)."

The Richmond studio's most important blues records were actually produced in 1929 for Paramount Records, the leading race label and a Gennett competitor. While constructing a new recording

Little Labels—Big Sound

studio at its Wisconsin headquarters, Paramount paid Gennett's Richmond studio $40 per side to produce master discs of its artists. During that period, two of Paramount's most popular blues musicians, Charley Patton and Blind Lemon Jefferson, recorded in Richmond.

Gennett Records was already struggling when the stock market crash of 1929 led to the Great Depression. The company had severed its record-pressing deal with Sears the year before, and the Electrobeam Gennett label barely made a ripple in the market. Harry Gennett, Starr Piano president and Fred's older brother, felt that the parent company should focus on pianos and its refrigeration supply division, so he discontinued the Electrobeam Gennett label in December 1930.

The entire record industry nearly collapsed in the early 1930s, as annual sales for records dropped from 104 million copies in 1927 to just six million copies in 1932. Still, Gennett Records issued limited quantities of blues and country discs on the Champion label, including exceedingly rare recordings by Sykes and Broonzy. Just before the Champion label was closed in late 1934, country legend Uncle Dave Macon, then 64 years old, traveled to Richmond with singer-guitarists Sam and Kirk McGee. Six marvelous sides of gospel and blues-flavored country music were issued, the last hurrah for the Richmond studio. While the Gennetts continued to use the studio up through the 1940s to produce hundreds of sound effects records for the radio industry, the studio's pioneering days were over.

To the horror of music enthusiasts, nearly all the original metal masters of Gennett recordings later disappeared over time. In the 1930s alone, Fred Wiggins had thousands of these metal discs loaded onto railroad cars and hauled away and sold for scrap. "Times were hard at Starr Piano, and the company may have needed cash to meet payroll," recalled Ryland Jones, an employee on the work detail that day. "The talk has always been that those metal parts would be worth a million bucks today, though I couldn't tell you what recordings were there. After that day, I don't think he [Fred Wiggins] ever looked back on the recording end of things again." [9]

By 1937, the Gennett family was embroiled in bitter business

17

disputes. Starr Piano had suffered huge losses during the Depression, which further exacerbated tensions between the five owners: Henry Gennett's widow, Alice; her sons, Harry, Clarence, and Fred; and her daughter, Rose Gennett Martin. After a family confrontation with their lawyers, Harry, Alice, and Rose took over Starr Piano. Fred and Clarence, while maintaining company assets, were removed from Starr Piano's daily operations. Tensions between the Gennett family members existed for years afterwards.

Fred Gennett and his sons created a small manufacturing company up the hill from Starr Valley, which sold steel products and refrigeration supplies. Their first employee was Fred's longtime friend, Fred Wiggins, who had helped put Gennett Records on the jazz map in the early 1920s. He died in Richmond in 1948. By 1952, the failing Starr Piano was closed. Within a year, brothers Harry and Clarence Gennett passed away. Decca, and later, Mercury Records, continued to lease space in the factory, where they pressed records for several years.

Fred Gennett, unrecognized during his life for preserving some of the earliest jazz on record, died in 1964 while living in a country home outside of Richmond. In his later years, he rarely mentioned the record label and avoided record researchers who sought detailed information. Even his obituary in the local newspaper failed to mention Gennett Records. "In his last years, he was a wonderful grandfather, always dignified in a white shirt and tie," recalled a grandson, also named Fred Gennett. "But we had no idea he was involved in recording all of these famous jazz players." [10]

Fortunately, those records live on. Gennett's NORK, King Oliver, Wolverines, and Jelly Roll Morton releases have been coveted by collectors in the United States and abroad since the 1930s. In 1935, American Decca Records reissued the Champion label, including Gene Autry's original sides on Gennett and Champion. Around the same time, England's Brunswick label reissued the 1922–24 Gennett jazz classics. During America's 1940s Dixieland jazz revival, Gennett's landmark jazz was reissued on various labels, such as Commodore and United Hot Clubs of America.

Since the 1950s, Gennett classics have been reissued numer-

18

Little Labels — Big Sound

ous times on vinyl albums, and later on compact discs (CDs), by such companies as Riverside, Jazz Classics, Fountain, Herwin, Olympic, Smithsonian, and Milestone. Since the 1960s, David Freeman's County Records in Virginia has reissued Gennett and Champion country vocal and string music. Gennett blues classics appear on anthology labels, especially Yazoo Records. With nearly all Gennett metal masters gone, the reissues depend upon finding good copies of original Gennett and Champion 78-rpm discs.

Today, Richmond's once bustling Starr Valley is an industrial ghost town with a handful of crumbling factory buildings, including a piano assembly building with a fading "Gennett Records" sign painted on the wall. The abandoned recording studio collapsed in the 1960s and was eventually hauled away. But not all was lost in Richmond. The Wayne County Historical Museum on Main Street near downtown has created an impressive Starr Piano/Gennett Records exhibit. Henry Gennett's lavish 1902 home on Main Street, for years a declining apartment complex, has been fully restored and placed on the National Register and is used for offices. The brick mansion hearkens back to a time long ago when Starr Piano was a national industrial power, the Gennetts were prominent Richmond citizens, and unknown jazz, blues, and country musicians passed through the small Indiana town on the road to musical immortality.

The New York Recording Laboratories — Port Washington, Wis. — Trade Mark Registered

Paramount

ELECTRICALLY   RECORDED

12909-A   Vocal
                Guitar Acc.

High Water Everywhere
Part I
(Patton)
Charley Patton
L59

Two / **Paramount Records**

"They were the off-side. They never was known."

—Paramount's H.C. Speir describing the early blues legends

H. C. Speir, a white store owner and talent broker in Jackson, Mississippi, walked through a world unknown to mainstream America in the 1920s. He scouted the city streets and farm tenant houses of the black South in search of itinerant blues players to audition for Northern record labels producing "race records." Speir typified the small fraternity of scouts involved in country blues recording, which peaked in the late 1920s. Through regular contact with his black customers, he knew what records they liked. Speir linked the record label executives, who generally knew nothing about black music, with the blues musicians hoping to record. He was also moved by the raw, emotional sound of black blues, a familiar sound to any rural Southerner at that time.

Speir's association with blues players at the bottom of the socioeconomic ladder was not deemed respectable by his peers, but it was good business. Living in the heart of Mississippi, he was within driving distance from the isolated black enclaves where country blues thrived. Many blues players auditioned at Speir's music and furniture store on a primitive 78-rpm disc recorder that he kept upstairs. Speir collected a finder's fee for the musicians he signed to Vocalion, Columbia, OKeh, Paramount, and other labels that sold race records. In return, his association with race labels, especially the small Paramount label in Wisconsin, kept him apprised of new 78-rpms to stock for his predominantly black clientele. He held no illusion of discovering national recording stars. "They were the offside," Speir said. "They never was known. They were not known to anybody." [1]

At least not then. It took decades for country blues musicians to earn widespread notice. The race record industry began in the early 1920s as a black niche market advertised through mail-order catalogs and black newspapers. Initially, most race 78-rpm discs featured female blues singers, vaudeville and minstrel performers, and jazz bands. By the late 1920s, however, race labels targeted Southern blacks with acoustic country blues or what was called "down home" music. The introduction of electronic recording technology in 1925 vastly improved the fidelity of country blues discs, which generally consisted of a solo singer accompanied by guitar or harmonica.

While viewed as racially insensitive today, Paramount's advertisements in African-American newspapers in the 1920s and early 1930s caught the attention of its "race records" audience.

While hundreds of titles by untrained blues players were issued, production runs were low. With few exceptions, the records provided the musicians little money or recognition. After the Great Depression decimated the record industry and killed the race records market, the surviving 78-rpm discs became tokens of a forgotten era.

When these early blues records were reissued on vinyl albums in the 1950s and 1960s, they helped to fuel a folk revival across America and Europe. Bob Dylan, Jimi Hendrix, Janis Joplin, Eric Clapton, Keith Richards, and other rock musicians were deeply inspired by these reissued recordings from the 1920s. Their new interpretations of old records provided far greater recognition for the blues originators than they ever enjoyed during their lives. The late blues pioneers Robert Johnson, Blind Lemon Jefferson, and Charley Patton, as well as others still living, were ultimately revered as rock pioneers.

The new awareness led field researchers to the South, particularly the Mississippi Delta south of Memphis, Tennessee, where a distinct blues style originated early in the century. They interviewed aging blues singers, their relatives, and early record scouts to compile a history that otherwise would have been lost. Up until the 1960s, many people incorrectly assumed country blues recording began with Library of Congress field sessions in the 1930s, unaware that it was a commercial activity the decade before. Finally, details surfaced on the first blues artists and on the defunct record companies that documented their work.

Among the most fascinating of these 1920s labels is Paramount, whose rare blue and black–labeled discs have a cult following with 78-rpm collectors. Company details were scant until researchers Stephen Calt and Gayle Dean Wardlow found surviving executives, scouts, and several of its artists in the 1960s. Paramount was never a leading record label, and its race records were often outsold by race releases from the larger labels, such as Columbia. Paramount also issued gospel, popular song, hillbilly, ethnic, and language records and also supplied discs for other labels, such as Puritan, Jewel, Oriole, Pathe, and Cameo.

However, Paramount recorded most of the decade's greatest blues musicians. Through resourceful talent scouts, such as Mayo Williams in Chicago and Speir in Mississippi, Paramount debuted the giants Ma Rainey, Jefferson, Patton, Skip James, Son House, and Blind Blake, among others. The label's string of successful releases by Jefferson and Blake in 1926 caused a shift in the race records industry from female singers to male singers. Paramount produced more than 1,000 different race record titles from 1922 to 1932, which appears to be about 20 percent of all race titles produced during the era. Production ranged from obscure black vaudeville and minstrel entertainers to celebrated Chicago-based jazz musicians, including Jelly Roll Morton, Joe King Oliver, and Freddie Keppard. The label's Depression-era discs capture the development of Delta blues, a distinct regional music that eventually influenced post–World War II Chicago blues and rock 'n' roll.

The rise of Paramount as a blues and jazz pioneer paralleled

Jelly Roll Morton, among jazz music's first great composers, debuted on the Paramount label in 1923. In 1923-24, he produced a significant body of piano solo works on the Gennett label.

24

Little Labels—Big Sound

that of its 1920s archrival, Gennett Records. Paramount was also a low-budget, sideline operation of a family-owned Midwest manufacturer, the Wisconsin Chair Company. The parent company was founded by Fred Dennett in the 1880s in the small, German-influenced Wisconsin town of Port Washington, about 30 miles north of Milwaukee. With access to prime timberlands and skilled European craftsmen, the company successfully produced furniture for home and business use. When several phonograph patents expired in 1915–16, Wisconsin Chair joined the legion of manufacturers entering the booming phonograph industry formerly dominated by Victor, Columbia, and Edison. Between 1914 and 1917, the number of phonograph manufacturers grew from a couple of dozen to more than 150.

Initially, Wisconsin Chair manufactured wooden phonograph cabinets for other companies. By the time World War I began, the company was producing and selling its own phonographs through a well-established furniture distribution network. In about 1917, Wisconsin Chair created the Paramount record label to promote its phonographs. Paramount was operated through a company subsidiary called the New York Recording Laboratories, a primitive recording studio in a 15-story office building on Broadway in Manhattan. Record-pressing operations were set up near the company's Port Washington headquarters in tiny Grafton, Wisconsin. Otto Moeser, a protégé of Fred Dennett, initially ran the record division, despite knowing little about the music industry. Like other New York–based labels at the time, Paramount found recording prospects on the countless Manhattan entertainment stages.

By the early 1920s, upstart Paramount faced the same challenges as its small competitors. Edison, Victor, and Columbia dominated the phonograph and record industry, produced superior quality discs, and had exclusive control of America's most popular acts. Also, the introduction of inexpensive home radios by the Crosley Radio Company in Cincinnati, Ohio, created a less expensive alternative to 78-rpm discs, causing an overall record sales slump. The small labels were forced to seek untapped consumer markets, which they found in the neglected black and white rural populations. New

25

York's OKeh label initially led by recording blues singer Mamie Smith, whose hit "Crazy Blues" in 1920 helped create the race label market.

Paramount was close behind. In 1922, Paramount diversified its catalog by first introducing a smattering of race records, including sides by blues singer Alberta Hunter, a popular theater performer in Chicago and New York and a former artist on the tiny, black-owned Black Swan label. Paramount, which had initially pressed 78-rpms for the Black Swan, ultimately purchased the company's metal master discs. Through its association with Black Swan, Paramount saw a potential in race records. It soon expanded its race catalog by recording in Chicago, which had America's largest black population. There, the label employed J. Mayo Williams, one of the young industry's first black entrepreneurs.

From 1923 through 1926, Williams helped to establish Paramount as a race label. The former Brown University graduate and football star worked briefly for Black Swan before managing Paramount's activities in Chicago. He also ran Paramount's Chicago Music Co., which held the publishing rights to the label's race tunes. Williams' education and business acumen, however, did not spare him from the indignities of segregation. He had to use the freight elevator, for example, to attend Wisconsin Chair executive meetings at a Wisconsin hotel.

Articulate, handsome, and resourceful, Williams had little rapport with the street-educated black entertainers he recruited and recorded. He recognized blues as part of his heritage, but preferred the sophisticated music of his college friend, the black stage performer Paul Robeson. Like Robeson, Williams also played professional football on the weekends in the newly formed National Football League with such struggling franchises as the Canton (Ohio) Bulldogs and the Hammond (Indiana) Pros.

Despite his disinterest, blues music became Williams' stock and trade with Paramount. Told not to involve himself with the label's white performers, Williams handled all facets of Paramount's Chicago race recording, such as scouting and auditioning performers, supervising recording sessions, and having songs formally arranged and copyrighted. Chicago was the perfect place for building Paramount's race records catalog. "By this time, so many [blacks] had come up here from the South and other parts of the country because Chicago was a music center," Williams said. "They'd bum rides, hop trains to get up here, any way they could get somebody to make a record." [2]

From his office in south Chicago near the famed State Street entertainment district, Williams auditioned many Paramount performers. Most recorded for a flat fee with little chance of receiving a royalty check. Williams held strong opinions regarding race recording. An educated African American, he was known to clean up dirty lyrics and require the proper pronunciation of words. Yet he discouraged black singers from using pop songs, demanding nothing but the blues. "In doing it that way I'd save a lot of embarrassment for myself, the company, and the person," he said. [3]

Because Paramount never owned a studio in Chicago, Williams held sessions at independent studios, including the Marsh Record Laboratories, a small operation on Chicago's South Wabash Street, owned by Orlando Marsh. (Marsh also produced his own local Autograph label, which recorded early black pianists Jelly Roll Morton and Clarence Jones.) Paramount performers often made a single visit to the Marsh Laboratories for a flat fee of $20 to $50, and Williams recorded as many songs as possible in a day. By the mid-1920s, Rainey, Ida Cox, and Charlie Jackson, among the many blues singers Williams recruited and recorded in Chicago, had established Paramount as a major race label.

One of the most influential of the 1920s female blues singers, Rainey had been performing on the black theater and tent-show circuit for 25 years when Williams found her at the Monogram Theater in Chicago in 1923. "After many years of appearing in theaters of the South, Ma Rainey went to New York — astounding and bewildering the Northerners with what they called queer music," stated a Paramount brochure. "She left and still they did not understand." [4] But with the success in the early 1920s of blues singers Mamie Smith on OKeh and Bessie Smith on Columbia, competing labels also sought female blues singers, and Rainey's day had arrived.

27

Paramount's advertisements in the *Chicago Defender* in 1923 announced the release of Rainey's 78-rpm discs with the headline "Discovered at Last — The Mother of the Blues."

In a raw style reflecting her Georgia background, Rainey belted out more than 100 sides for Paramount. "See See Rider" and "Ma Rainey's Black Bottom" became classics. Paramount even issued a special souvenir 78-rpm disc of Rainey's "Dream Blues" with her photograph on the label. Draped in flashy clothes and jewelry, Rainey toured constantly in the 1920s with original material and experienced musicians while promoting her Paramount releases. Despite the label's bad fidelity, Rainey's voice sounds full and clear on these old discs.

Another Williams discovery, Ida Cox, billed "The Uncrowned Queen of the Blues," recorded more than 70 sides for the label in the 1920s. Cox, a Tennessee native, was a stylish performer whose songs often contained amusing sexual overtones. Papa Charlie Jackson, a New Orleans Creole and street performer signed to Paramount by Williams in 1924, sang humorous material while accompanying himself on the banjo. Recording more than 60 sides for Paramount, much of it his own material, Jackson became one of the first male black singers to achieve widespread success in the 1920s race records industry.

Paramount showcased Rainey, Cox, and Jackson with some of America's best black jazz musicians, who were also featured on the label as solo acts. Paramount jazz releases featured King Oliver's Creole Jazz Band of 1923, with cornetist Louis Armstrong and clarinetist Johnny Dodds, Morton, Thomas Dorsey, Jimmy Blythe, and Cow Cow Davenport. While recording for Paramount in New York, Rainey was backed by members of the famed Fletcher Henderson Orchestra. Paramount also recorded cornetist Freddie Keppard, an early New Orleans jazz hero, who accompanied Jackson on several recordings.

Despite Paramount's impressive roster, selling race records was a challenge. Most of black America in the 1920s lived in the rural South, often great distances from retail centers. Many Southern stores refused race records in fear of attracting too many black customers. Some refused to display the records, and would pull them out from under the counter only upon request. Paramount's media advertisements appeared in the *Chicago Defender,* a popular black newspaper with readership beyond the city. The advertisements instructed customers to fill out a printed form with their selections and mail it to the Wisconsin pressing plant. Selling records by mail, like Sears & Roebuck, helped Paramount reach its remote customers. Paramount also recruited independent door-to-door salesmen with promises of "a big commission on every sale." Black railroad porters working out of Chicago were known to distribute Paramount discs in the South as a sideline business during their travels. An important source for wholesale business was Artophone in St. Louis, a leading distributor of music instruments and 78-rpm discs. Artophone distributed Paramount race records to Southern furniture and music store operators.

One of these store owners became a vital source of talent for Paramount. In 1925, R. T. Ashford, a Dallas store owner and Paramount dealer, contacted the label's new marketing director, Art Laibly, about a blind singer and guitarist performing for pocket change on Dallas street corners. The singer knew one of Ashford's employees, a pianist named Sam Price, and had a following among local blacks. Ashford figured that many of his customers would buy records by this local celebrity. At the time, small record labels commonly heeded the musical suggestions of its individual retailers. On Ashford's urging, Laibly arranged for recording dates with the blind singer in Chicago. Between his first releases in 1926 and his mysterious death in 1929, Blind Lemon Jefferson recorded almost 100 sides for Paramount, as well as discs for OKeh. With a repertoire of Southern blues, hymns, prison dirges, and folk songs, Jefferson became the most commercially successful male blues singer of the 1920s.

Jefferson's extensive output on Paramount has been exhaustively analyzed. His precise guitar playing, characterized by melodic finger-picking, was rare in early country blues. He possessed a strong, clear singing voice, and his songs spoke to black listeners in a powerful way. Other than many biographical details contained in his

Blind Lemon Jefferson, country blues singer discovered while performing on Texas street corners, gained a huge following with black record buyers in the late 1920s with Paramount Records.

original lyrics, very little is known about his vagabond life. He was born in the late 19th century in eastern Texas. Apparently, he learned to play the guitar as a way to perform on street corners, at picnics, private parties, dances—wherever he could pick up some loose change and a free drink. Paramount's promotional material depicted his rise to stardom with melodramatic flare:

"Can anyone imagine a fate more horrible than to find that one is blind?" said a Paramount brochure. "To realize that the beautiful things one hears about—one will never see? Such was the heart-rending fate of Lemon Jefferson, who was born blind and realized, as a small child, that life had withheld one glorious joy from him—sight. Then environment began to play its important part in his destiny. He could hear—and he heard the sad hearted, weary people of his homeland, Dallas—singing weird, sad melodies at their work and play, and unconsciously he began to imitate them—lamenting his fate in song. He learned to play a guitar, and for years he entertained his friends freely—moaning his weird songs as a means of forgetting his affliction. Some friends who saw great possibilities in him, suggested that he commercialize his talent—and as a result of following their advice—he is now heard exclusively on Paramount."[5]

Soon after his debut on Paramount with the back-to-back songs "Got the Blues" and "Long Lonesome Blues," Jefferson's stream of successful releases changed race recording. The number of male singers entering recording studios rose after Jefferson's arrival, just as Mamie Smith's hits for OKeh prompted the female blues invasion in the early 1920s. But the industry's search for the "next Jefferson" rarely produced a performer with his originality and sheer technical ability. Jefferson's more enduring recordings for Paramount include "That Black Snake Moan" and "Match Box Blues."

Following Laibly's success with Jefferson, Paramount debuted another blind male blues singer named Blind Blake in 1926. Williams apparently found the Florida native performing on Chicago streets. Little is known about Blake, though Paramount claimed he somehow "absorbed Florida's sunny atmosphere in his music, disregarding the fact that nature had cruelly denied him a vision of outer

31

things."[6] Blake became a label mainstay, producing dozens of sides over the next several years. Sunny disposition aside, Blake was a sophisticated guitar player whose finger-picking melodies drew from ragtime, popular song, and early jazz.

Despite Williams' success as a talent scout, his relationship with Paramount gradually deteriorated. Williams claimed decades later that Laibly considered himself a more superior source of race talent. "When he [Laibly] found out there was big money in this field, he became envious and jealous of me, because I had a better 'in' than he had," Williams claimed. "And then he decided that he wanted to get into the recording end of the business and kinda bugged me a great deal, and harassed me and so forth."[7] By 1927, Williams stopped representing Paramount. For a brief period, he managed the day-to-day operations of the short-lived Black Patti label, a race label financed by Fred Gennett at Gennett Records. Later in the 1920s, Williams worked for Jack Kapp at Brunswick Records as a talent scout. He maintained ties to the music business in Chicago on and off over the next couple of decades.

Toward the end of the 1920s, Paramount faltered as home radio affected the entire record industry. The label's primary sales were in Mississippi, Alabama, and Arkansas, behind the distribution arm of Artophone. Then Artophone stopped handling 78-rpm discs. Paramount shut down its New York studio and its Chicago presence waned. Ma Rainey stopped recording, leaving blind singers Blake and Jefferson as Paramount's mainstays in the race market. A rural Kentucky native who played the fiddle as a child, Laibly expanded Paramount's "old time" country catalog, pressing the same recordings for several discount labels. Meanwhile, Laibly searched the South for blues singers, relying on local retailers and distributors to serve as scouts. In the years before Paramount's 1932 shutdown, Laibly unknowingly made music history by prolifically recording the Mississippi Delta blues.

Few whites in the 1920s knew the isolated Delta blues scene like H. C. Speir, the Mississippi talent scout who had a feel for the music and knew where to find musicians. Or often, the singers simply arrived unsolicited at his store for an audition. In 1929, he drove from

Jackson to the large Dockery plantation in the state's rural northeast to meet a favorite of local blacks, a diminutive, light-skinned singer and guitarist named Charley Patton. Around 1900, Patton's parents moved from southern Mississippi to the fertile, northern Delta region to work as sharecroppers on the large, self-contained plantation owned by the Dockery family. (The plantation had its own workers' quarters, company store, and currency.) Influenced as a youth by the plantation's blues singers, Patton became a popular traveling singer at black parties and juke joints—anywhere he could earn enough money to avoid the drudgery of farm labor. A drinker, gambler, womanizer, and troublemaker (vices that would define the blues player), Patton was also a flamboyant entertainer. He sang and sometimes held the guitar over his head or between his legs, to produce enough melody and rhythm to get folks dancing and hollering.

Patton fascinated Speir with his originality. Speir wired Laibly and strongly suggested a recording session in mid-1929. At the time, Paramount had recently abandoned recording in Chicago and was constructing its own studio in Grafton, Wisconsin, on the second story of a drafty factory across the road from the company's pressing plant. Temporarily without a studio, Paramount contracted Gennett's Richmond, Indiana, studio to produce master discs at $40 per side. Laibly provided Patton a ticket for the 800-mile train ride to Indiana and Speir pocketed a finder's fee. Then, one of the great blues recording sessions occurred on June 14, 1929, as detailed in the Gennett recording ledgers. Patton, a seasoned performer in his 30s with a vast repertoire, produced 14 sides that day. The informal Richmond studio was known for its prolific sessions, and its arrangement with Paramount rewarded productivity. Patton's discs were unlike any music recorded before. He shouted often unintelligible lyrics, but in a powerful voice with expressive phrasing. His percussive guitar playing reflected the manner in which he entertained at Delta gatherings.

Paramount's first release from the session in late 1929 featured "Pony Blues," a song Patton had known for years, and "Banty Rooster Blues." Paramount's *Chicago Defender* advertisements declared, "What he can't do with a guitar ain't worth mentioning." Patton's

33

new relationship with Paramount in late 1929 coincided with the death of Jefferson in Chicago. Unconfirmed reports had Jefferson dying of a heart attack and in a snowstorm. Paramount issued a special disc with a blues song "Wasn't It Sad About Lemon" on one side, and a spoken sermon, "Death of Lemon Jefferson" on the other. In actuality, with Jefferson gone, Paramount apparently hoped that Patton could revive its lagging race record sales and recorded 40 sides by the Delta singer in just one year.

Paramount worked all the angles in promoting Patton's material. A song called "Prayer of Death" was issued under a religious pseudonym, Elder J. J. Hadley. Another release, "Screamin' and Hollerin' the Blues," listed the performer as "The Masked Marvel," with an advertisement depicting a black man in a tuxedo and a Lone Ranger's mask with the catch line "Guess Who He Is?" The promotion of Patton's lament to cocaine addiction, "Spoonful Blues," was illustrated with a well-dressed Patton sitting dejectedly in a fancy restaurant, being served a bowl of soup.

With Paramount declining swiftly in the early 1930s, Patton traveled to Grafton with a local fiddler to produce several sides. The best seller from the session was apparently "High Water Everywhere," about the 1927 Mississippi River flood that turned the Delta into a shallow lake 300 miles long. After traveling through the Delta to find Patton later that year, Laibly organized the singer's last Paramount session. Patton recruited guitarist Willie Brown, his longtime performing partner, pianist Louise Johnson, and Son House, a former preacher and convicted murderer who had begun singing and playing blues guitar with Patton in the late 1920s.

Chauffeured by a non-drinking acquaintance, the four musicians piled into a car for a long, wild ride to Wisconsin. The trip was marked by arguments, bootleg whiskey, and House's sexual liaison with Johnson, as House claimed in interviews with music researchers Stephen Calt and Nick Pearls in 1966. The music they recorded was fresh and original, with each of the players singing songs, supported by the others. Perhaps most remembered are Patton's "Moon Going Down," with Brown supporting on guitar, and House's powerful "Preachin' the Blues," which details how the blues corrupted him.

Little Labels—Big Sound

During the early 1930s, Laibly recorded other Delta artists recommended by Patton and Speir, such as Skip James, Tommy Johnson, Ishman Bracey, and a popular Jackson, Mississippi, singing group, the Mississippi Sheiks. However, the record business was collapsing. Paramount had ceased advertising in the *Chicago Defender* by then and dozens of Paramount's Delta blues records from 1929 to 1932 barely sold. Paramount helped to make Patton something of a music celebrity with Mississippi blacks, but few original copies of his records have survived, and some have never been found. That these musicians were ever recorded is amazing. Laibly's failed attempt to sustain the label's race records sales by recording unknown Delta players starkly illustrated the perils of waging a music revolution.

Laibly was eventually fired. He briefly sold busts of George Washington to Minnesota schools before pursuing a career in insurance. In mid-1932, shortly after releasing a few Patton sides in limited quantities, Wisconsin Chair closed the Paramount division and abandoned the Grafton studio and production plant, leaving the equipment inside to rust. Some Paramount master discs were sold to Starr Piano; most were sold as scrap copper. A Wisconsin Chair employee reportedly used Paramount metal masters to build a chicken coop. Tens of thousands of Paramount discs in storage in Grafton were sold to a New York dealer for one penny each. During the 1930s and early 1940s, Wisconsin Chair was gradually dismantled. The Paramount recording equipment was eventually stored away, and the pressing plant and studio were torn down. Whatever ledgers existed on the label's sessions were destroyed.

In 1934, an ailing Patton and his wife recorded several uninspired sides for the American Record Company in New York. A few months later, he died of heart disease in the Delta at the approximate age of 43. By then, the Depression made 78-rpm blues records a luxury few blacks could afford.

But the Paramount legacy lived. In 1942, John Steiner, a chemist and music enthusiast from Milwaukee, approached Wisconsin Chair executives about buying remnants of Paramount. "For $2,000, I picked up some metal master plates, a couple of test pressings, and

35

basically a lot of good will in obtaining the rights to the music they had copyrighted," Steiner said. "They also pulled out the old rusty recording equipment, but I had no use for it. Paramount had always issued interesting music, and, having lived nearby, I had a special interest. They were more than glad to collect a little money for what was left of its music operations. They had no interest in it whatsoever." [8]

During the 1940s, Steiner and business partner Hugh Davis reissued Paramount releases on their "S.D. Records" label. Meanwhile, a coterie of white collectors of blues and jazz 78-rpm discs actively purchased Paramount race records at bargain prices. By the 1950s, some of these collectors, which included talent scout John Hammond, Bill Grauer, Orrin Keepnews, Harry Smith, Pete Whelan, Nick Pearls, and Bernard Klatzko, used original 78-rpm collections to produce vinyl album compilations of Paramount race releases on such small labels as Riverside, Folkways, Origin Jazz Library, and, in the 1960s, Yazoo Records.

Through these reissue anthologies, Paramount recordings became part of the 1960s rock and folk repertoire. On his debut album in 1962, Bob Dylan recorded Jefferson's 1927 Paramount release, "See That My Grave's Kept Clean." Jefferson's "Match Box Blues" was the inspiration behind early rock star Carl Perkins' 1957 hit song, "Matchbox," covered by the Beatles in 1964. Cream, the English rock trio with Eric Clapton on lead guitar, recorded Patton's "Spoonful Blues" as well as Skip James' "I'm So Glad."

With new interest in their early Paramount recordings, James and House were "discovered" and billed as blues legends on the 1960s folk and jazz circuit. Members of the rock band Canned Heat found James living in near-poverty in Mississippi. Even though he had been out of the music scene for decades, he was booked at the Newport Folk Festival and other major musical events until his death in 1969. House had been living in obscurity for years in Rochester, New York. Upon his discovery in 1964, he also toured extensively in the United States and Europe as the public fascination with early Delta blues artists surged.

Meanwhile, researcher Gayle Dean Wardlow uncovered the

obscure Paramount story. Through Ishman Bracey, Wardlow learned of Laibly's role. Advanced in years and retired from an insurance career in Illinois, Laibly offered limited details. "Clearly, Laibly did not appreciate the (blues) music," Wardlow said. [9] But the interview led Wardlow to H. C. Speir, who was still living in Jackson. Speir, 69 years old when Wardlow first met him in 1964, lived a quiet life, growing large tomatoes in his garden and selling real estate on the side. He owned no records from the blues singers he signed. "He [Speir] was puzzled by my interest," Wardlow said. "To him, it was just a business from a long time ago. He was going to church now, and he didn't want to talk about that blues music aspect of his life."

Over several visits, Wardlow played a variety of Paramount blues records for Speir, including the Patton classics. Upon hearing them, Speir opened up with important details. "He said these blues guys would drink anything with alcohol in it, so they always had a certain smell," Wardlow said. "But he was very fond of blues music, and he really liked Charley [Patton]. When I told him the music was getting big, he just grinned. I kept telling him that he [Speir] was now a part of that history, but he didn't see it that way."

Speir, who died in 1972, may have felt differently had he lived for the 1995 opening of the Rock and Roll Hall of Fame and Museum in Cleveland, Ohio, where country blues is properly celebrated as a cornerstone of rock music. This certainly pleases Steiner, whose foresight in the 1940s preserved the Paramount blues legacy. "It is wonderful that a small group of people around the world are still fascinated by Paramount and the country blues music," he said. "That's why these recordings are so wonderful. This music just goes on forever." [10]

DIAL
R E C O R D S

11-4-47
Contemporary
American Music   1021-A

SCRAPPLE FROM THE APPLE

CHARLIE PARKER QUINTET
CHARLIE PARKER ....Alto Sax
MILES DAVIS ....Trumpet
DUKE JORDAN ....Piano
TOMMY POTTER ....Bass
MAX ROACH ....Drums
(D-1113)

Three / **Dial Records**

"Bird [Charlie Parker] was the easiest of all musicians to record. It was just a matter of getting him there."

—Ross Russell, Dial Records owner

At a 1994 Christie's auction in central London, 85-year-old Ross Russell sat astonished as collectors bid on artifacts of Charlie "Bird" Parker, the legendary jazz saxophonist who died in 1955 from dissipation at age 34. Signed notes, a recording contract, assorted correspondence, and other incidentals kept for decades by Parker's widow each fetched thousands of dollars. Competing against Japanese investors, the mayor of Kansas City, Missouri, Parker's birthplace, telephoned a bid of nearly $300,000 for a plastic alto saxophone used briefly by Parker, who was notorious for pawning his horns for drugs.

The white-haired Russell attended simply as a curious spectator. Since he personally knew the saxophonist and wrote the definitive Parker biography, *Bird Lives*, Russell recounted in his mind some of the countless little items discarded decades ago which might have made him a millionaire that day. No matter. The significance of Parker is his music, and, to that end, Russell preserved a treasure trove. In fact, the worldwide fascination with Parker's music is attributable in no small way to Russell's Dial Records. In the mid-1940s, Dial was among a handful of tiny labels that preserved and disseminated "bebop," the revolutionary jazz movement spearheaded by Parker, Dizzy Gillespie, Thelonius Monk, and their contemporaries in New York City.

The impact of bebop, the cornerstone of modern jazz, continues today. But when Russell organized 16 jazz recording sessions for his fledgling Dial label during 1946–48, bebop was largely ignored or derided by the public, by the media, and even by the jazz establishment. Despite public indifference, Russell pressed forward with releases by bebop pioneers Parker, trumpeters Gillespie, Miles Davis, Fats Navarro, and Howard McGhee, drummer Max Roach, trombonist J. J. Johnson, tenor saxophonists Dexter Gordon, Wardell Gray, and Teddy Edwards, and one of jazz's most popular pianists, Erroll Garner.

After two challenging years recording jazz in Hollywood and New York City studios, Russell focused on 20th-century classical composers, who challenged traditional musical conventions in the same way bebop turned the jazz world upside down. Russell recorded works of modernists Arnold Schoenberg, Igor Stravinsky, Bela Bartok, and others before abandoning the Dial label in 1954.

Today, Dial is revered foremost for recording Parker, one of the century's most important musicians. His seven sessions for Dial in 1946 and 1947 produced 35 releases and more than twice as many alternate takes, resulting in some of his best sessions backed by skilled sidemen. The Dial releases thoroughly document Parker's improvisations, as well as his compositions, which were often based on the chord progressions of standard Tin Pan Alley songs. An intuitive musician, Parker developed his compositions on the bandstand, never bothered to commit them to staffed paper, and played from memory in the recording studio. The Dial sessions debuted such future Parker classics as "Ornithology" (which resembles the standard "How High the Moon"), "Scrapple from the Apple," "Yardbird Suite," and "Klactoveesedstene."

Looking back, Russell marveled at how pure luck was at work. He was operating a small music store in Hollywood in late 1944 just as Parker and Gillespie were introducing bebop music in Los Angeles–area clubs. Russell's young customers (whom he affectionately called "hipsters") demanded the hard-to-find bebop records and transformed the store into a modern jazz hangout. They helped Russell to recognize the profound change underway in jazz. After watching Parker's late-hour sets at Billy Berg's nightclub in Hollywood, Russell realized that he had stumbled upon a musical genius. "I would have never understood Bird's music if not for the hipsters in the store," he said. "I was in the right place at the right time." [1]

Russell created Dial in early 1946 to record Parker and other bebop musicians. Bankrolled by Marvin Freeman, a Los Angeles attorney and fellow jazz enthusiast, Russell recorded and pressed shellac 78-rpm discs and, later, some of the first 33-rpm jazz albums, which sold in small quantities to jazz music stores throughout the country. Despite struggles to cover overhead expenses, Russell believed that Dial records could become as influential as the 1920s jazz discs by Louis Armstrong, Jelly Roll Morton, and King Oliver that Russell had collected since the early 1930s.

Exercising great foresight, Russell made his best effort within a

Little Labels — Big Sound

limited budget to capture the moment. "When I found myself with Bird under contract, I made it my business to learn everything possible about producing a good sound in a recording studio," he said. "I tried to use a top engineer in a top studio. I did have a strong feeling that the music was for posterity. A very strong feeling. Marvin [Freeman] didn't share it. Nor did the reviewers. And as they used to say on The Street [Manhattan's 52nd Street], Bird was the easiest of all musicians to record. It was just a question of getting him there." [2]

No one knew better than Russell. His business affairs with Parker were tumultuous. Exclusive contracts were repeatedly violated. Parker produced a notarized document awarding half of his Dial royalties to Emery Byrd, a heroin peddler who operated out of a wheelchair and later received his Dial royalty checks at San Quentin Prison. When Parker was committed in 1946 to a California mental institution, Russell negotiated his release. Because of Parker's dependency on drugs and alcohol, his disposition in the studio ranged from inspired and focused to temperamental and incoherent. His Dial sessions are legendary not only for the music, but for the difficult circumstances under which he was recorded.

The one constant was Parker's brilliant playing. Russell worked around Parker's personal difficulties and went to great lengths to ensure a studio setting conducive to creative performance. Unlike many larger commercial labels, Russell gave Parker freedom to choose the material, sidemen, and even the recorded takes to release. In the recording studio, Russell tried to recreate the atmosphere of a night club such as The Three Deuces or Birdland. "I became convinced that good sessions were organized before musicians arrived at the studio," he said. "At each session, if things had gone well, something special had been captured." As for the haunting quality commonly attributed to Parker's Dial releases, Russell also hears it. "It's all part of great art," he said, "and comes along once in a lifetime." [3]

For Russell, to preserve landmark jazz was only fitting. Long before he tried jazz producing, Russell was among California's first serious collectors of early jazz 78-rpms. He was born in 1909 in Glendale, California, and graduated from Glendale High School in 1926. Later, he enrolled as a premedical student at the University of

41

California, Los Angeles (UCLA). The 1929 stock market crash wiped out the family savings, along with his chances for a medical career. Inspired by a collection of works by 19th-century French novelist Honore de Balzac, Russell eventually returned to UCLA to study English in hopes of becoming a writer.

At UCLA, he discovered jazz as well as literature. Two upper-classmen, Marvin Freeman and Campbell Holmes, had become jazz fanatics while studying a year at Heidelberg University in Germany. "They spoke of jazz as a beautiful flower growing among the weeds at America's back doorstep," Russell said. "They exposed fellow students to heavy doses of jazz but there were few takers. For some reason, the music got through to me."[4] In the early 1930s, small groups of jazz enthusiasts on college campuses, particularly at Ivy League schools, avidly collected 1920s hot jazz records on such defunct labels as Gennett, OKeh, and Paramount. The Great Depression nearly wiped out every label recording jazz, forcing students to rummage in second hand stores or go door-to-door in black neighborhoods to seek out hard-to-find 78-rpms from the 1920s. These avid collectors were critical in developing the earliest jazz discographies.

Russell helped to form a jazz record collectors club at UCLA. "There were four of us, regarded as lunatics by the other students," Russell said. The loose network of collector organizations nationwide was visited regularly by another Russell, William Russell, later an important jazz historian, who traveled the country with a Chinese puppet show, spread the news of recent 78-rpm finds in junk shops and used furniture stores, and furnished lists of artists to collect. The lists included Louis Armstrong, Bessie Smith, Jelly Roll Morton, Bix Beiderbecke, Clarence Williams, and Eddie Condon. "Collecting 'hot jazz' [in the United States] was very different from collecting in Europe," Russell said. "There, the major labels had experts to study lists of new releases on American labels and make arrangements for their release on the His Masters Voice, Parlophone, and Brunswick labels in Europe. All the overseas collector had to do was study the catalog and ask for the records in a shop."[5]

In America, the jazz record collector had to be much more of

Little Labels—Big Sound

a treasure hunter. Driving his Model T Ford, Russell scouted Los Angeles for old jazz records. At a Spanish music store, he discovered shelves of mint-condition OKeh records, including several of Armstrong's classic small-group recordings. An electrical supply store in Burbank, with a logo of the defunct Gennett Records in the window, led Russell to a former dealer who had stored in a barn crates of classic Gennett sides by Oliver and Beiderbecke's Wolverines. "I claimed I was a trumpet player and was trying to play like Bix," Russell said. At one antique shop, Russell walked out with a stack of old jazz records purchased for a penny apiece, but not before leaving his mark. "While going through these records in the back of the room, I suddenly had to urinate," he said. "Fortunately, I found a large antique Chinese vase nearby. " [6]

When Russell graduated from UCLA in 1932, jobs were scarce. He worked for a couple of years as a caddie while submitting his work to the pulp publishers that supplied the magazine and book racks of drug stores in 1930s America. In 1937, Russell became friendly with jazz band leader Luis Russell, who invited the young writer to travel with the band on a tour of one-nighters in Northern California. The band was fronted by Armstrong, along with other jazz giants, including Pops Foster, Red Allen, and Zutty Singleton.

In 1938, after three years of rejections from publishers, Russell received a check for $125 in payment for three short stories; he immediately headed East and eventually settled in New York. During the cross-country trip, he stopped in Chicago and toured the southside clubs to find his idols: Johnny and Baby Dodds at the New Plantation Club, trumpeter Roy Eldridge at the Three Deuces, clarinetist Jimmie Noone in the pit band at a strip joint. The high point—hearing the Earl Hines Orchestra at the lavish Grand Terrace Ballroom—left a lasting impression. When he arrived in New York's Greenwich Village, Russell naturally gravitated to Milt Gabler's famed Commodore Music Shop, home of the Commodore jazz label and a Manhattan mecca for jazz musicians and fans.

The United States entered World War II in 1941 just as Russell, now 32, was becoming an established writer. He joined the U.S. merchant marine to beat the draft and wound up as a radio officer. He spent a couple of days on a life raft after his ship was hit by a German torpedo in the Barents Sea. Upon leaving the service, Russell returned to California and worked briefly for Lockheed Aircraft. In June 1944, he used the $5,000 earned from 14 months in New Guinea to open the Tempo Music Store on Hollywood Boulevard. His personal phonograph was built into a listening booth to play a jazz record inventory bolstered by his personal stock of prized 78-rpms.

Russell's vision of a traditional jazz specialty store, stocked with discs by Louis Armstrong and Duke Ellington, was soon altered by his young customers. A new breed of jazz had been born in the early 1940s during jam sessions in Minton's Playhouse in Harlem, and the bebop movement soon spread to the string of clubs along New York's 52nd street. Russell's West Coast patrons sought the lightning-fast, rhythmic bebop being recorded by a new generation of jazz players on New York's tiny Comet, Guild, Continental, and Savoy labels. As Russell stocked the hard-to-find discs, Los Angeles bebop fans and musicians adopted the store. When Gillespie and Parker, New York's leading bebop players, arrived on the West Coast with a sextet in December 1945, the Tempo Store newsletter heralded their extended engagement at Billy Berg's on Vine Street near Hollywood Boulevard. While their performances confused many in the audience, bebop found support among musicians.

Emulating Milt Gabler's Commodore concept of a store-based jazz record label, Russell in January 1946 created the first West Coast label specializing in bebop. Russell's college mate, Freeman, supplied the extra capital to launch the venture and suggested the label's name. It was inspired by his favorite 1920s literary magazine, *The Dial*, edited by poetess Marianne Moore. Wally Berman, a regular at Russell's store, developed the distinctive Dial logo.

Russell and Freeman created Dial with the best intentions but knew nothing about recording sessions. It showed at the session in February 1946 organized by pianist George Handy, whose grandiose scheme was to organize a super all-star band fronted by Gillespie, Parker, and Count Basie's lead tenor saxophonist, Lester Young, who was Parker's musical role model. At the rehearsal, Young never appeared. At the recording session, Parker was also a no-show. With

Little Labels—Big Sound

studio time already paid, the session was saved in the nick of time when Gillespie was found at the Dunbar Hotel in the African American section of Los Angeles. Gillespie arrived by taxi within the hour, with all of Billy Berg's band except Parker.

Russell salvaged his investment by recording Gillespie and his sidemen on five numbers before they left for New York. "None the less, the session got out of hand," Russell said. "Despite precautions, hippies filtered into the studio, sat on the floor, lit up, confused the engineers. The results were so-so, although everyone, especially Diz and Al Haig, played well. After that, I made it my business to keep hangers-on, dope heads and parasites out of the studio. I also made a survey of studios in Los Angeles. The city had the best studios in the world thanks to the many technical developments that followed the introduction of sound films." [7]

Gillespie returned to New York, but Parker stayed behind. In March 1946, a Tempo Music customer brought him to Russell, and a recording contract with Dial was signed. Russell assured Parker complete artistic freedom and provided him with a $100 advance on royalties from the store cash register. That month, Parker organized a septet with the young trumpeter Miles Davis flown in from New York to fill the spot vacated by Gillespie. "He [Parker] wanted someone with a more relaxed style who played in the middle register, like me," Davis said. "I found out after I got to Los Angeles." [8]

During the three-to-four-hour session at Radio Recorders studio in Hollywood, Parker debuted three originals, "Moose the Mooche," "Yardbird Suite," and "Ornithology," along with Gillespie's "A Night in Tunisia." The latter three songs became jazz standards. Davis' smooth lines complemented those of Parker, but the trumpeter muffed several takes on which Parker played his best. Performances were still recorded on lacquer discs from which metal stampers were fabricated, for overdubbing through the use of audio tape had not begun. "Davis's constant fluffs required additional takes, sometimes as many as five, before Parker was satisfied with the result," Russell said. "Ironically, Parker often played his most inspired and original solos on the first take." [9]

Davis knew he had caused problems, but he forever resented

45

Dial Records

*Jazz trumpeter Dizzy Gillespie and Dial owner Ross Russell in
California in 1946. A jazz record collector-cum-record producer,
Russell produced some of America's first "bebop" jazz recordings
on a shoestring budget.*

Russell for pointing them out. "I never did get along with him
[Russell] because he was nothing but a leech who didn't never do
nothing but suck off [Parker] like he was a vampire," said Davis in his
autobiography, *Miles Davis*, in which he derides Russell and
others. [10]

 While Russell's first session with Parker was artistically exhila-
rating, it left him extended financially. From the several thousand
dollars advanced by Freeman, Russell had produced two 78-rpm
discs, one by Parker, and the other by Gillespie. Strapped for money,
Russell cut down on new releases but continued to seek recording

Little Labels—Big Sound

opportunities. Parker's back-to-back "Ornithology"/"A Night in Tunisia" disc would sell several thousand copies in its first year of release, but Parker frustrated Freeman and Russell with a legal document instructing that half of his royalties be paid to Byrd, Parker's heroin connection.

Russell resumed recording activities in the summer of 1946, with an excellent small-group session by Woody Herman sidemen, headed by trombonist Bill Harris. He then booked Parker in July at the MacGregor Transcription Studios in Los Angeles. Suffering from heroin withdrawal, drinking heavily, and alienated by the West Coast, Parker arrived in disastrous shape for what drummer Roy Porter later called the most catastrophic recording session in jazz history. Providing no original songs as promised, Parker headed a quintet of local players, including Porter and trumpeter Howard McGhee, through standard tunes familiar to the group.

After consuming Phenobarbital provided by Freeman's physician brother, Parker labored through the songs. On "Lover Man," Russell had the engineer record the entire struggle, thus preserving Parker's mental and physical anguish before he was removed from the studio. Even though Russell has been criticized for decades for issuing the performance, it continues to fascinate listeners because despite Parker's condition, his musical instincts pulled him through. That evening, firemen rescued a naked Parker from his burning hotel room. (Earlier, he had appeared naked and incoherent in the hotel lobby.) He was eventually committed to the psychiatric ward at Camarillo State Hospital outside Los Angeles. Davis later summed up Parker's situation: "When Bird left New York he was a king, but out in Los Angeles he was just another broke, weird, drunken nigger playing some strange music." [11]

By late 1946, with Parker still in Camarillo, Russell had become Dial's sole owner. He sold the music store and used the proceeds to compensate Freeman for his investment in Dial. With six 78-rpm discs now in the Dial catalog (four by Parker and one each by Gillespie and Harris), Russell pushed sales hard to generate additional income and working capital. Meanwhile, he worked with Camarillo authorities to release his marquee artist. After Parker was

Dial Records

released in Russell's custody in early 1947, he joined trumpeter Howard McGhee's band at the Club Hi De Ho in Los Angeles.

In February, Russell promptly organized two sessions for Parker. The first had him backed by Erroll Garner's trio (in Los Angeles at the time) on Parker's "Bird's Nest" and "Cool Blues." The session was organized to record a Parker acquaintance, singer Earl Coleman, whose voice was reminiscent of Billy Eckstine. After Coleman struggled for two hours to produce "Dark Shadows" and "This Is Always," Parker and the Garner trio quickly shifted gears and recorded the easygoing instrumental sides. "Bird was then in the best health of his life, dried out, well fed, well rested, off drugs and alcohol, and this is the Bird that might have made hundreds of records," said Russell. [12]

Later that month, Russell surrounded Parker with some of the best West Coast players available, including McGhee, guitarist Barney Kessel, bassist Red Callender, pianist Dodo Marmarosa, and tenor saxophonist Wardell Gray. As Russell detailed in *Bird Lives*, the band waited at MacGregor studios while McGhee found Parker asleep, fully clothed in a bathtub. The session produced three McGhee originals and Parker's "Relaxin' at Camarillo," one of several original Parker tunes titled by Russell. It was based on a 12-bar blues line Parker scribbled on a music pad while in a taxicab. It so confused the band during rehearsal that he trashed the score and played the melody on his horn until the band learned it. (Incidentally, Russell never thought to retrieve from the studio trash can the crumbled paper with Parker's notations, one of the few times Parker committed musical ideas to staffed paper.)

With his February sessions completed, Parker returned to New York. Russell would follow him there later in 1947 to resume recording, but first he produced West Coast sessions for Los Angeles tenor saxophonists Wardell Gray and Dexter Gordon. Later to become an all-time giant on tenor, the 24-year-old Gordon returned to his hometown of Los Angeles in 1947 to escape the rigors of New York and touring. "Dexter was one of the leading tenor men of the bop era and had a big, robust sound," Russell said. "He was also hopelessly addicted to heroin." [13] In early June, Gordon recorded "Mischievous

Charlie "Bird" Parker, one of jazz's most influential musicians, recorded many of his best small-group disks on Ross Russell's fledgling Dial label. This photo is from a 1947 Dial session in Los Angeles.

Dial Records

Lady" and "Lullaby in Rhythm" with a quintet including trombonist Melba Liston, later to become a recognized jazz composer.

Russell then teamed Gordon with Gray on "The Chase," a six-minute tenor saxophone duel of chase choruses pressed on both sides of a 78-rpm disc. Gordon and Gray, who frequently dueled on the bandstand, are a perfect study: Gordon's bold, rhythmic sound contrasts with Gray's smoother, softer tone. With the possible exception of Parker's "Ornithology," Gordon and Gray's "The Chase" was Dial's best seller. (Gray, who died in Las Vegas in 1955 under mysterious circumstances, has been largely forgotten by the jazz world, as is his influence on Gordon and others in Los Angeles during the late 1940s.)

Dial also recorded Gordon with a trio on several cuts including an original, "Bikini," a bluesy bop tune now included in the Smithsonian Institute's Collection of Classic Jazz. On Gordon's final session for Dial, in December 1947, he teamed up in MacGregor's studio with another local tenor player, Teddy Edwards. Similar in approach to "The Chase," the Edwards and Gordon collaboration on "The Duel" is another fun tenor battle, supported by pianist Jimmy Rowles, bassist Red Callender, and drummer Roy Porter, one of Dial's regulars.

After Russell arrived in New York in late 1947, further sessions with Parker appeared bleak. Parker, who violated his Dial contract by recording with Savoy Records, planned to let the contract expire while his manager shopped for a major label. All bets were off when a dispute between the American Federation of Musicians (AFM) and the record companies resulted in another recording ban set to begin on January 1, 1948. A panicky Joe Glaser, Parker's manager, fearful that his client would have no record releases available during the ban, negotiated a revised Dial contract, which resulted in three outstanding sessions in late 1947.

Russell organized the sessions between late October and Christmas using the Parker quintet working the Three Deuces nightclub: Davis, pianist Duke Jordan, bassist Tommy Potter, and drummer Max Roach—one of the best jazz groups ever recorded. Russell again dug deep into his limited resources and rented time in the quality

WOR studios in Manhattan. Russell and Doug Hawkins, a music graduate of Julliard and the session's engineer, paid careful attention to technical details, such as placing a high-impedance microphone near Roach's cymbal to capture the calming hiss one now associates with a classy jazz ballad.

During two sessions in October and November, the group recorded a dozen songs, including six Parker originals, most notably "Scrapple from the Apple," "Dexterity," and "Klactoveesedstene," one of the few originals Parker titled himself. Many consider Parker's improvisational treatment of George Gershwin's "Embraceable You" to be his finest moment in the studio. Three more Parker originals were produced on his final Dial session in December. The leading bebop trombonist J. J. Johnson joined the group on such numbers as the bluesy "Bongo Beep" and "Quasimado," an interesting Parker original that was never part of his regular repertoire.

Parker never recorded again for Russell. He soon joined record producer Norman Granz (operator of the Clef, Mercury, and Verve labels) and remained with him for the remaining seven years of his life. Granz showcased Parker in a more commercial vein with outstanding results, but Parker listeners tend to prefer his Dial and Savoy small-group dates.

About a year after Parker's last Dial session, Russell stopped recording jazz but remained active in the jazz record business. The 1948 introduction of vinyl albums enabled Russell, who had recorded everything Parker played in the studio, to release the many alternate takes of Parker's recordings. Dial was one of the first jazz labels to sell albums at a time when consumers were just beginning to accept the new format. Russell transferred his Dial master discs onto reel-to-reel tape, from which pressing stampers were produced to make the albums. From 1948 to 1954, Russell issued several bebop albums, in both the 10-inch and 12-inch format.

Loaded with Parker's alternate takes, the albums helped to spark a scholarly assessment of his work, which continues unabated. Where Parker's Dial 78-rpm discs were the most polished group efforts, the outtakes first released on the Dial albums probe Parker's creative process. Many of his most imaginative improvisations are on

51

recorded efforts relegated to outtakes because a sideman, often Davis, had flubbed. Other times, different takes of the same song were equally excellent. For example, in the Smithsonian's Collection of Classic Jazz, two different takes of Parker's "Embraceable You" on Dial show Parker's contrasting improvisational approaches.

Russell also used the album format to compile fascinating Parker finds beyond his Dial sessions. He bought the brilliant Comet Records masters of 1945 with Parker and Gillespie backed by pianist Teddy Wilson, vibes player Red Norvo, and bassist Slam Stewart. During a 1947 private party in California celebrating Parker's release from Camarillo, a jam session with Parker was recorded on a home disc cutter by the party's host. Russell copied the original homemade discs, which appeared on a 1953 Dial album.

When viewed today with the benefit of 40 years' hindsight, the original album cover designs tend to belie the music's stature. One cover takes a Parker photograph, superimposes a cartoon beret on the side of his head while he stares at a primitive drawing of a blackbird perched in a tree. "You couldn't get away with a sophisticated cover showing the artist," Russell said. "The cartoon cover was the thing."[14] Then again, Russell possessed a sense of humor. A record collector himself, he issued the ultimate collectable, the "Crazeology" 78-rpm disc from Parker's last Dial session in 1947. Side "A" captures a processing glitch when the selected take was inadvertently etched twice onto the master disc. Russell was intrigued by the slight sound delay it caused and released it, along with a side "B" that crams excerpts of Parker's solos from three "Crazeology" rejected takes. Parker considered it demeaning, and Russell himself later wondered if it was such a good idea.

In 1949, Russell produced the Dial contemporary classics catalog. His releases of modern composers received great reviews but sold poorly. Shortly before dropping the Dial venture altogether, Russell issued albums of calypso music he recorded on tape during a Caribbean vacation.

By 1954, Russell was fed up with the recording business and New York. He sold his Dial jazz masters for $25,000 to the Concert Hall record company in what he called "the greatest mistake of my

Little Labels—Big Sound

life." Concert Hall had sold mail-order vitamins and planned to start a jazz mail order club. The project bombed, and Concert Hall soon sold the Dial tapes to Crowell Collier. A court battle between Concert Hall and Crowell Collier ensued and the tapes were impounded. Some were ultimately lost or stolen.

Over the next several years, the out-of-print shellac Dial 78-rpms and vinyl albums became collectors items, while the Parker material on Dial resurfaced in chaotic order on various obscure labels worldwide, including Doris Parker's short-lived Parker label. Bootlegging of the material was rampant. "Had I kept it [the Dial catalog] intact, I could have lived on it the rest of my life," Russell said. [15]

While the business of jazz frustrated Russell, jazz writing and research remained central to his varied writing and teaching activities in the post-Dial years. Up through the 1970s, his firsthand accounts of Parker and bebop were published in U.S. and European music magazines. In the late 1950s, Russell wrote a beatnik jazz novel, *The Sound*. His exhaustive study, *Jazz Style in Kansas City and the Southwest*, was published in 1967 by the University of California Press and stayed in print for 20 years. In 1971, Russell produced a reunion of Kansas City jazz giants, called Kansas City Revisited, at the Monterey Jazz Festival.

His research into Kansas City jazz, along with his Dial experience, form the bedrock of his most important work, *Bird Lives*, a biography of Parker published in 1973. As with Russell's Dial experience, critical success was tempered by financial setbacks. His book's royalties were used to defend a plagiarism lawsuit filed by the widow of Robert Reisner, author of the less-enlightened 1962 biography, *Bird: The Legend of Charlie Parker*. In addition to writing and promoting jazz, Russell over the years dabbled in public relations (including publicity director for a dragstrip!), advertising, photography (he shot photos for a bullfight monthly), as well as teaching writing and music history.

Meanwhile, Russell's Dial masters enjoy a life of their own, thanks to English jazz aficionado Tony Williams. In the 1970s, he created a reissue label, Spotlite Records, which compiled Parker's

53

Dial sessions in proper chronological order. No simple task, the effort required the enthusiastic assistance of Russell, who provided dates, background, locations, matrix numbers, and a few still unreleased Parker masters. The result, a six-album series on the Spotlite Masters label, became a major event in the jazz world and rekindled interest in Parker with a new generation.

In the late 1980s and early 1990s, Parker's Dial masters continued to be packaged in album and compact disc (CD) format. For example, Warner Brothers in 1988 issued "The Very Best of Bird," a double album featuring 26 Dial sides. It capitalized on Clint Eastwood's film production on Parker, "Bird," whose soundtrack included Dial's "Lover Man" track. Currently, the complete Dial compilation of Parker, produced by Williams, is available on a four-CD package issued on Stash, "The Complete Dial Sessions," a fitting tribute to Russell's perseverance.

The demand for Russell's original Dial 78-rpms and albums continues to grow, now selling in mail auction for well over $100 each, not only because of their rarity and significance, but also because Russell pressed them with quality materials. Dial 78-rpms have held up quite well; most Dial albums were pressed in pure vinyl, and surviving copies in good condition are quite playable.

In 1980, Russell and his wife moved to South Africa, and later, Austria. During that time, he placed his personal archive with the Harry Ransom Humanities Research Center at the University of Texas in Austin. The mammoth archive includes thousands of jazz albums and 78-rpm discs, hundreds of jazz books, countless articles, taped interviews, and his correspondence with major jazz scholars. The collection also contains Dial business records and other related documents.

When the author corresponded with Russell in 1997, he was in his late-80s and as enthusiastic as ever. He lives in the small southern California desert town of Niland, at the foot of the Chocolate Mountains, where his jazz research continues. Though his most recent book was published in 1973 ("a shameful record" he said), Russell is working on a detailed study of the bebop era, as well as a book profiling such colorful jazz figures as Mezz Mezzrow, Lester Young,

Billie Holiday, and Albert Ammons. In mid-1994, Russell was warmly greeted as a speaker at the annual convention of the International Association of Jazz Record Collectors, held in London. While there, he attended the Christie's auction featuring Parker memorabilia, where he was instantly recognized by the Parker cognoscenti. He also visited The Rising Sun pub, a venerable stomping ground in London for Parker fanatics, where Russell was treated like royalty by the jazz collectors.

Russell continues to faithfully correspond with jazz researchers seeking his recollections. The one-time fanatical record collector is a part of the jazz history he so cherishes. As for being subjected to the same old questions? "Never get tired of talking about Bird," he said.

Dial Records

Four / **King Records**

"Nobody wants to hear that noise."

—Syd Nathan upon hearing James Brown's first demo recording

On February 4, 1956, James Brown and the Flames made history in a former ice factory in Cincinnati, Ohio, that housed King Records. Across the South, Brown had earned a name for himself as a loud and unearthly howler of rhythm and blues. Record producer Ralph Bass invited him to King, thinking the raucous singer would complement the company's growing R&B roster on its Federal subsidiary label. By then, King was a leading R&B and country record company, a fact not lost on Brown.

When they arrived at 1540 Brewster Avenue, in Cincinnati's working-class Evanston neighborhood, King looked anything but regal. The turn-of-the-century King factory, painted battleship gray, was located in a shabby area. Inside, cold air penetrated brick-walled rooms, record presses clanked and wheezed, and the halls were thronged with odd characters. As Bass escorted the band through a maze of corridors and cubbyholes, the young men walked past photographs of King's stars: saxophonist Earl Bostic; organist Bill Doggett; the Royals; Moon Mullican, king of the boogie-woogie piano; and other known and unknown faces from the Deep South, Northern ghettos, and hardscrabble mountains. They were a potpourri of race, talent, and unlikely ambitions. Brown wanted to be one of them.

In the studio, the Midnighters wailed some wild R&B number, while a couple of hillbilly singers dressed in wide-brimmed cowboy hats smoked cigarettes and strummed guitars on the loading dock. When their turn came, Brown and the Flames approached the microphones for a full-scale assault. King president Sydney Nathan ("Little Caesar," as Brown later called him) was shocked. "What in the hell are they doing? Stop the tape," Nathan yelled from the control room. "That doesn't sound right to my ears. What's going on here?" Turning to Bass, Nathan said, "The demo was awful, and this is worse. I don't know why I have you working here. Nobody wants to hear that noise." [1]

Distracted by another crisis, Nathan left the studio, giving the band time to complete four songs: "Please, Please, Please," "I Feel That Old Feeling Coming On," "I Don't Know," and "Why Do You Do Me Like You Do." Before long, "Please, Please, Please" sold a

A young James Brown early in his career with King Records in Cincinnati. Brown broke onto the national scene in 1956 with "Please, Please, Please," a million seller for King's Federal label. For several years, Brown was King Records' leading attraction.

Little Labels—Big Sound

million copies for Federal. The "noise" Nathan detested in 1956 became one of his main attractions. But he had many others. That same year, Doggett's "Honky Tonk" on King soared to number two on *Billboard* magazine's pop chart, and *Cashbox* awarded the "R&B Record of the Year" to King's Little Willie John for "Fever." During this period, the Cincinnati plant was pressing 20 million records annually.

King Records was clearly a reflection of Nathan's vision and personality. He was an entrepreneur who could grab the world by the throat and drag it his way. His presence was unmistakable: short, fat, and bald, with a gravelly voice that boomed through walls and echoed down brick corridors. He wore Coke-bottle glasses with heavy black frames and waved a missile-sized Cuban cigar as he talked. (Even in portraits, he is seen holding a cigar.) He installed loudspeakers throughout the office and factory, and he bellowed orders from his desk telephone. Nathan's massive desk was shaped like a 45-rpm record sawed in half. He often wore no shoes, and employees were accustomed to seeing him slide along the concrete hallways in suit, tie, and socks.

Employees remember Nathan as a saint, genius, and curmudgeon. He could be all three on any given day, but they admired his originality. He was an intense competitor who browsed in pawnshops to test his bargaining power. He verbally battered any human obstacle between him and success. Somehow, he always found the breath to keep shouting. Those he couldn't inspire, he intimidated into action. Yet at the same time, he worried about the label because he felt responsible for his employees. Knowing the industry's volatile nature, he operated frugally. He saved money by recycling vinyl and refused to join the Record Industry Association of America (RIAA) because he didn't want to pay the annual fee (or reveal sales figures). As a result, many of Brown's hits on King were not RIAA-certified million sellers.

Nathan was not only an operator, but an innovator, during his 25-year reign at King. He hired blacks for important company positions. He set up his own distribution system to bypass powerful independent distributors, and he created an in-house factory to

59

record, master, press, design, print, and distribute records. His small army of salesmen sold records from their car trunks. Nathan produced crossover country and R&B hits and developed one of the first company studio rhythm sections, a concept soon adapted by other labels, such as Sun. Early on, Nathan used electric instruments on country sessions. He published a country music fan magazine in the late 1940s and campaigned to change the derogatory appellation of "hillbilly music" to country music. He founded Lois Music (BMI), a financially successful song publishing company. He used the pseudonym Lois Mann to collaborate on numerous hit songs, including "As Advertised" and "Signed, Sealed and Delivered" by Cowboy Copas.

Under one roof, Nathan built a truly self-contained independent record company. The King plant had everything he needed, except the equipment to make shipping cartons. A singer could walk into King in the morning and leave that night with a new record in his hands. "Mr. Nathan used to say, 'All you need to get into the record business is a desk, a telephone, and an attorney.' But he built a solid company because he could do everything in-house," said Jim Wilson, King's longtime sales manager. "He didn't have to answer to a lot of other companies or people." [2]

Even from the beginning, Nathan was never one to answer to people. He was born on April 27, 1904, in Cincinnati, and grew up suffering from asthma and poor eyesight. He quit school in the ninth grade. During the Depression years, he tried everything: drummer in a local speakeasy, busboy, pawnshop clerk, shooting gallery owner, wrestling promoter, amusement park concessionaire, radio salesman, jewelry salesman, and traveling jukebox supplier. He dreamed of owning his own business. In the late 1930s, he opened a small wholesale radio shop on West Fifth Street. The business survived as the city poked its head out of the Depression. Then one night at the Beverly Hills Supper Club, across the Ohio River in northern Kentucky, Nathan encountered a jukebox outlet owner who owed him six dollars.

"Six bucks meant more to me in 1938 than $1,600 now," Nathan said. "I saw the fellow with a gorgeous blonde. I figured he

Little Labels—Big Sound

would be in the next day with my six bucks. He didn't show. For three weeks in a row I saw him at Beverly with the same babe. Finally on the dance floor I grabbed his shoulder and told him, 'If you can afford Beverly, you certainly can afford to pay me.' He turned red, blue, and green. He said he didn't have it. The next day he came into the shop and offered me 300 hillbilly, western, and race records from his jukeboxes at two cents a platter. I figured I could sell each of them for 10 cents and get back my six bucks. I took him up. The first afternoon I made $18." [3]

Selling individual records soon bored him. He sold the shop to relatives and moved to Miami to be near his brother, physician David Nathan. He opened a new photo-finishing business, but 1939 brought snow and sleet to the Sunshine State and killed his venture. Back in Cincinnati, he opened a record store in a poor neighborhood and bought enough records to see him through World War II. "During the war, records were hard to get," he said, "and naturally I thought of a brilliant idea, that I could get some hillbilly singers and cut some records, and somebody would press them for me. I thought it would be as easy as all that." [4]

Nathan targeted the neglected race, country, and western music markets, which he called the "music of the little people," the Appalachians and blacks who had bought his used records. In those days, Cincinnati industries drew Appalachians and blacks like a magnet. The city was partly rural, partly urban, and different musical styles and people converged. Bolstered by World War II and internationally known industries, including Procter & Gamble and Cincinnati Milling Company, industrial Cincinnati thrived. For Appalachians, it promised steady work, and the hills were only a few hours away by car. The largest migration occurred from 1940 to 1970, when Cincinnati attracted 100,000 new people, mainly from Appalachia.

Culturally, Cincinnati was steeped in country music. In the 1930s, 50,000-watt WKRC presented regular hillbilly shows. WLW, with an incredible 500,000 watts until the federal government ordered power reduced to 50,000 watts, nationally broadcast hillbilly and western shows featuring Gene Autry, Red Foley, and other well-known artists. From 50,000-watt WCKY, hillbilly and blues programs reached the East Coast. Cincinnati's hillbilly radio talent included Homer and Jethro, Bradley Kincaid, Chet Atkins, Joe Maphis, the Delmore Brothers, Lloyd "Cowboy" Copas, Curly Fox and Texas Ruby, Lazy Jim Day, the Girls of the Golden West, and Lulu Belle and Scotty Wiseman. The music was foreign to Nathan, but his record customers wasted no time educating him.

By November 1943, he persuaded WLW performers Louis M. "Grandpa" Jones and Merle Travis to accompany him to nearby Dayton, Ohio, to record for what became the King label. They took the chance, knowing that major labels signed few country singers. King's first record was "The Steppin' Out Kind" and "You'll Be Lonesome Too," with Jones and Travis billed as the Shepherd Brothers. Few copies of the poorly pressed discs were usable, but Nathan didn't mind. He placed the company's slogan, "The 'King' of Them All," next to the crown logo on the early labels, and he turned out new and sturdier discs. Nathan also convinced friends and relatives to invest in his dream. He hired workers, obtained and rebuilt hard-to-find record-pressing equipment, rented a vacant part of the Brewster Avenue plant, and started seeking distributors.

Soon, Grandpa Jones was recording in Cincinnati, Hollywood, Chicago, or wherever Nathan could find a good studio and the right musicians. Jones saw his 78-rpm discs in jukeboxes everywhere, wobbling on turntables like old tires. "I went into the Army later in '44, after I cut 'It's Raining Here This Morning,' a pretty big record." Jones said. "Well, Syd got me to sign a contract. I didn't care. I just wanted to pick on a label. He really fixed me: he made the contract out so I would get only 5/8 of a cent a side. That was about a cent and a half a record. I sold so many records that one time my check for three months was over $1,000. So he made all the money, and I didn't. But he didn't cheat me out of the publicity. The records helped me." [5]

Nathan soon signed local radio singers and musicians for King sessions. He built his recording studio on Brewster Avenue in the late 1940s. The King house band, a forerunner of Nashville's studio session teams, included: Louis Innis, bass and rhythm guitar; Zeke

Little Labels—Big Sound

Turner, electric guitar; Kenneth "Jethro" Burns, mandolin; Jerry Byrd, steel guitar; and Tommy Jackson, fiddle. Nathan also used such impressive guitarists as Henry "Homer" Haynes, Billy Grammer, Hank Garland, and Jackie Phelps, pianist Shorty Long, and harmonica player Wayne Raney. Red Foley played bass on a Grandpa Jones session.

Early hits recorded at King included: "I'll Sail My Ship Alone" and "Mona Lisa" by Moon Mullican; "Heart of Stone" by the Charms; the naughty R&B hits "Big Ten-Inch Record" by Bull Moose Jackson; "Work with Me Annie" and "Annie Had a Baby" by the Royals; and "Sixty Minute Man" by Billy Ward and the Dominos. (Over the years, Ward's lead singers included Jackie Wilson and Clyde McPhatter.) A few years later, Hank Ballard and the Midnighters (formerly the Royals) recorded the original version of "The Twist" there, as well as the hit "Finger Poppin' Time."

The strange musical and racial juxtaposition at King progressed under Henry Glover, a black trumpet player hired as King's chief producer, arranger, and songwriter. Nathan found him in Lucky Millinder's big band, where Nathan also discovered jump singer Wynonie Harris and other singers and employees. By the late 1950s, Glover and King producers Ray Pennington, Louis Innis, Gene Redd, and Ralph Bass had forged new sounds. Among the five, probably Glover was most comfortable with King's musical diversity. The Alabama native appreciated hillbilly, blues, and big band music. His original songs wove universal themes easily interpreted by hillbilly and R&B singers. Glover wrote bandleader Sonny Thompson's 1952 hit "Drown in My Own Tears," sung by Lulu Reed, and then recorded it with others. Nathan appreciated Glover's ability and rewarded him with his own publishing company, administered by Lois Music. Glover thus became one of the first black record executives.

"I'll confess that we didn't think we were doing anything remarkable. It's just that we had both types of artists, and when a song happened in one field, Syd Nathan wanted it moved into the other," Glover said. [6] "In many ways, he was a remarkably open-minded

The brash Syd Nathan, founder of King Records, produced an enormous body of hillbilly, honky-tonk, R&B, and soul music for America's post–World War II working class. King was one of many independent labels which laid the groundwork for the rock 'n' roll revolution.

man. He perceived this wonderful notion of American music as not being segregated into different styles, but one big cross-ethnic whole. He did that because it was a way to make money." [7]

In 1946, Nathan recorded "Hillbilly Boogie" and "Freight Train Boogie" by the Delmore Brothers, who, years earlier, were a hit act for RCA's Bluebird label. Their new King records brought the duo back into national prominence, but this time with a harder edge. In 1949, Alton and Rabon Delmore recorded their biggest King hit, "Blues Stay Away from Me," and under Nathan's guidance, their faster music became a precursor to rockabilly. Meanwhile, King's sales increased as Nathan signed more hillbilly performers, includ-

Little Labels—Big Sound

ing Cowboy Copas, Hawkshaw Hawkins, Wayne Raney, Clyde Moody, Homer and Jethro, Hank Penny, Jimmie Osborne ("The Death of Little Kathy Fiscus"), Zeb Turner, the Lightcrust Dough-boys, the York Brothers, the Carlisle Brothers, and a local television singer, Charlie Gore.

Through King, Cowboy Copas became a top national hillbilly star, recording such hits as "Filipino Baby" and "Tragic Romance." For a time, he shared equal concert billing with Hank Williams. The quiet Copas, a native of Appalachian Adams County, Ohio, became good friends with Nathan. A regular performer on WLW's "Boone County Jamboree" program in Cincinnati, Copas left the area in 1946 to join Pee Wee King's band and secure a place on the Grand Ole Opry in Nashville. But he continued to record hits for King, including "Hangman's Boogie," "The Tennessee Waltz," and "Strange Little Girl." In 1963, he was killed in a plane crash that also took the life of Patsy Cline.

Key to King's rise was Nathan's instinctive ability to market records. He advertised judiciously in the trade magazines and sold records through non-traditional outlets, such as general stores and 32 company sales branches. The branches enabled King to circumvent slow-paying, autocratic independent distributors. Nathan's offbeat operating procedures extended to the studio and offices. Before the civil-rights movement changed America, King mixed musicians and hired blacks for office and factory jobs. By the late 1940s, 20 percent of King's workforce was black.

Nathan had formed Queen Records in 1945 primarily to record black music, but, a year later, eliminated the label to focus on King. Nathan's earliest black performers included Bull Moose Jackson ("I Love You, Yes I Do"), Sonny Thompson ("Long Gone"), Ivory Joe Hunter ("Jealous Heart," "Guess Who"), and Lonnie Johnson ("To-morrow Night"). In 1947, Nathan acquired the established DeLuxe label and operated it as a King subsidiary. He also purchased R&B masters from Miracle Records in Chicago. In 1950, he formed Federal Records, primarily as a vehicle for R&B producer Ralph Bass, who came from independent Savoy Records. Before leaving for Chess Records in 1958, Bass brought to Federal the Dominoes, Ike

Turner, Johnny Otis, the Five Royales, Little Esther, Etta James, Little Willie Littlefield, Johnny "Guitar" Watson, Jimmy Witherspoon, and other blues and R&B performers.

By 1949, King was selling six million records a year, including 250,000 copies of Wayne Raney's number one country hit "Why Don't You Haul Off and Love Me." It was cut in King's new recording studio in Cincinnati, where Wynonie "Mr. Blues" Harris cut "Good Rockin' Tonight," a Lois Music song later covered by Elvis Presley. It is difficult to imagine Harris, a legendary R&B wild man, bumping shoulders with pickers from the Kentucky hills. But the King studio overcame racial barriers. The emerging "Cincinnati Sound," bluesy music tinged with a country feel, combined black and Appalachian heritages. It impressed the Indiana guitarist Lonnie Mack, a King sideman whose blues-rock style culminated in his 1963 Fraternity Records hit, "Memphis," based on the Chuck Berry original.

Most King releases were produced in the austere 35-by-20 foot studio in Cincinnati. For convenience, Nathan built it next to a loading dock. Porous white soundproofing tiles covered concrete block walls, and light fixtures hung from 25-foot ceilings. Although as dark as a garage, the studio produced a clear and funky sound, with depth and presence impossible to define. Ray Pennington, a King producer, attributed the studio's "live" sound to a combination of musicians and engineering know-how. "We ran a bass directly to the board," he said. "Many other studios didn't pick up on that until later. I think the studio itself was a big part of the King 'sound,' but in those days we had top musicians to go along with the studio." [8] In some cases, the musicians added to the studio's ambiance. Country singer Jimmie Logsdon remembered arriving in the studio immediately after James Brown's band completed a session. "Smoke was so thick you could cut it with a knife," he said. "Wine bottles were laying all around. It set the mood for me." [9]

Because Nathan published many of the songs his artists recorded, he often produced cover versions in pop, country, and R&B. By the mid-1950s, the company released polka, rockabilly, doo-wop, R&B, bluegrass, country, western swing, big band, comedy, pop, jazz, gospel, and even lush instrumentals leased from European labels for release on King International. The company's Royal Plastics division, led by Nathan's investor and second cousin, Howard Kessel, pressed custom orders for other labels and individuals.

By 1956, with hillbilly record sales declining, King emphasized black music, producing Little Willie John's "Talk to Me, Talk to Me," and other hits. The label's blues artists included guitar wizard Freddie King (whose King LPs greatly influenced 1960s British rock musicians such as Eric Clapton) and Earl Bostic, a King mainstay who played sax, clarinet, and flute. The Oklahoma native attended Xavier University in New Orleans before joining Hot Lips Page and Lionel Hampton. Bostic formed his own band in 1944. His biggest King hit was "Flamingo." He died in 1965, still a King favorite.

Bostic's keyboard counterpart, Bill Doggett, recorded the single "Honky Tonk," which sold more than four million copies. An R&B standard during the 1950s, "Honky Tonk" became one of King's bigger hits and influenced the early rock bands. Doggett never played a solo on the record, and the session was an afterthought. He followed it with such chart hits as "Slow Walk," "Ram-Bunk Shush," and "Soft." Other black artists on King over the years included Wilbert "Kansas City" Harrison, John Lee Hooker, the Swallows, Tiny Bradshaw, Roy Milton, Sticks McGee, Eddie "Lockjaw" Davis, Eddie "Cleanhead" Vinson, Champion Jack Dupree, Bubber Johnson, Donnie Elbert, Charles Brown, the Checkers, Annisteen Allen, and California saxophonist Big Jay McNeely.

As Nathan developed an impressive roster of R&B, blues, and hillbilly musicians, he also hired able A&R (artist & repertoire) men to find songs for them. In 1958, he brought in Hal Neely, an executive at Allied Records in New York, to supervise most of King's departments. Neely helped rebuild the King studio and pressing plant by installing a new stereo board and tape system and doubling the plant's capacity for manufacturing albums. Neely also reinvigorated King's country output. He signed new artists, such as the Stanley Brothers, and reactivated much of the old catalog. On Neely's advice, Nathan in 1961 purchased Bethlehem Records, a New York jazz label, bringing masters by Nina Simone and Mel Torme to King. "When I took over King in 1958, many of the old masters were still on glass and acetates, all stored away on a balcony in a hot warehouse," Neely recalled. "Some were on metal matrix. My first project was to build a temperature-controlled vault. There was no other good, full record of the old masters in the vault, especially the war-years' glass masters. We had one engineer who did nothing but rewind reels of tape."[10]

While Neely improved King's daily operations, Nathan spent much time in the Miami Heart Institute in Miami Beach. Nathan and his company began facing difficult times. The major labels, suddenly wiser, had invaded the country and R&B markets. Rock had taken hold, and the labels scrambled to promote their own versions of Elvis Presley. In 1955, King ventured into rockabilly and scored a top 10 hit with "Seventeen" by a former country band called Boyd Bennett and His Rockets. But with the exception of an occasional hit, the company's rock records made no inroads, and King was forced to concentrate on R&B and country.

By the early 1960s, Nathan wanted to run the company's daily operations again. He faced a difficult task; airplay was harder to obtain for his records, and the major labels had moved into his market. King continued to hit with James Brown's records, but the company struggled to find other million-selling performers. To survive, Nathan distributed other independent labels. The more successful ones included Beltone, a pop label in New York that hit the top 10 with Bobby Lewis's "Tossin' and Turnin'" and "One Track Mind," and 4 Star, a country label in Los Angeles that brought King the top 30 pop hit "Hot Rod Lincoln" by Charlie Ryan & the Timberline Riders and such performers as the Maddox Brothers and Rose and Ferlin Husky.

Nathan had proven fallible. He had little success in pop and rock music; neither could he make stars of the vocalists Otis Redding, Joe Tex, Dave Dudley, Al Grant (Guy Mitchell), Steve Lawrence (he signed before he turned 18), the Platters, April Stevens, Bruce Channel, Billy "Crash" Craddock, Mac Curtis, and Trini Lopez, among others. When Nathan needed big names, he signed older groups, including the Ink Spots, and acquired early masters by Patsy Cline and other performers at the height of their careers.

Little Labels — Big Sound

In the 1960s, James Brown clearly became King's main attraction. He experimented freely in the studio, and his peculiar brand of music continually frustrated Nathan, who held strong opinions on what was acceptable music. Nathan would walk into the studio, hear Brown recording, and start yelling. Brown defended his projects against Nathan's tirades and, on occasion, paid for recording sessions himself to prove their worth. For example, Brown's 1962 landmark LP "Live at the Apollo," a million seller for King, was initially financed by the singer.

Despite the tumultuous relationship, Nathan made Brown a legend. King was a working artist's label, a blue-collar music machine, and it served Brown well. Brown asked Nathan to indulge him, and this indulgence resulted in more than 30 hit records from 1956 to early 1968. While their professional relationship alternated from grudging affection to dislike, they maintained a respect for each other, in part, based on their mutual ambition. Nathan would claim that if Brown followed his advice, he'd eat in better restaurants and wear fine clothing. During the early 1960s, Brown grew dissatisfied with King and recorded for a competing label, which led Nathan to pursue legal action for breach of contract. The dispute was soon settled with Brown staying with King but maintaining artistic control over his recordings.

In 1965, Brown recorded a funk song called "Papa's Got a Brand New Bag." Again, Nathan hated it, but it became Brown's first international hit. Then Brown cut "I Got You (I Feel Good)" at Nathan's favorite independent studio, Criteria Sound in Miami. Nathan cursed louder than ever, but still gave Brown his creative freedom. No matter how foreign Brown's music sounded to him, Nathan knew that both black and white kids loved the records. By the mid-1960s, Brown, now proclaimed by King as "Soul Brother Number One," sold millions of records, just as he predicted to Nathan during their studio shouting matches. "Night Train," "Cold Sweat," "It's a Man's, Man's World," "Try Me," "I Can't Stand Myself (When You Touch Me)," and other Brown records were pressed in the King plant, and elsewhere when demand rose.

As the 1960s drew to a close, Nathan's heart condition worsened. The illness kept him from the office for extended periods and his recording empire suffered. Sales branches closed, forcing King to use the often unreliable independent distributors. By then, the majors were dominating the country music market, descending on its stars, ballpoint pens in hand. Race records had broken out of the ghetto and into mainstream America; the stars and the stars-to-be no longer had to work through King.

On March 5, 1968, Nathan died of heart disease in Miami at age 63. His death put family members in a quandary. "It's sad to see a dynasty like King die," Ray Pennington said, "but I don't think anybody else was capable of keeping it going. Syd had a special way of seeing talent in people."[11] Investors sold the company to Hal Neely, who by then was working for Starday Records in Nashville. Neely bought all King music and publishing assets, contracts, and properties for $1.75 million, and formed a new company called King Records of Ohio, Inc. He then merged King with Starday to form Starday-King Records Inc., which controlled 22,000 song copyrights and 20,000 audio masters.

In late 1968, the owners sold the company to Lin Broadcasting Corporation. Both labels continued to release records under their own names, and James Brown opened his own office at the King plant in Cincinnati. He placed a marble top on Nathan's desk and added an engraved metal plaque: "I'll Always Remember The Man, S. Nathan."

In 1971, Neely purchased from Lin all Starday-King assets and contracts for $3.5 million in cash. He sold James Brown's personal services contract, which had seven years to run, and the singer's masters to Polydor for $1 million and his share of jointly owned publishing companies to Polydor for $376,000. He then formed a new firm, Tennessee Recording and Publishing Company, with partners Fred Bienstock, a music publisher; and songwriters-producers Jerry Leiber and Mike Stoller. Neely operated the company from the Nashville office. Bienstock administered the publishing companies in New York. Leiber and Stoller produced the records.

"The new partnership was not a happy one," Neely said. "It did not work. Conflicts of interests and personalities. Neither party would sell to the other. In early October 1973, I sold my interests in a bizarre turn of events on the flip of a coin. I lost."[12] Neely said he was surprised when his former partners quickly sold the Starday-King masters, catalog, contracts, and property to Moe Lytle of Gusto Records in Nashville. As the pieces of Nathan's kingdom were dispersed, his studio employees scattered across the country and continued to make hits for other companies. The King factory in Cincinnati was sold and its studio equipment was sent to Nashville. Most of King's other early performers have long since retired or died. An exception is Brown, who, after serving a prison sentence in South Carolina, continues to shout into his 60s.

For more than 20 years after his death, Nathan was largely a forgotten man, both in Cincinnati and within the recording industry. During the label's reign, the local establishment snubbed King as a local oddity owned by a tough-talking Jew who recorded hillbillies and Negroes with such strange nicknames as Moon, Ivory Joe, Hawkshaw, Curly, Grandpa, and Bull Moose. The former King factory in Cincinnati became a neglected musical shrine. Visible from Interstate 71 near downtown, the gothic-style bunker was for years a maintenance hub for United Dairy Farmers, a chain of dairy convenience stores. A 20-foot cow stood in the parking lot near a mountain of red and blue plastic milk crates.

However, Nathan's status was revitalized in the 1990s with the creation of the Rock and Roll Hall of Fame and Museum in Cleveland, Ohio. The Hall's burgeoning membership includes several musicians and producers from King, including the 1996 induction of Nathan. King is clearly a beneficiary of one of the Rock Hall's missions to identify rock's origins. The Rock Hall pays tribute to the early African-American R&B and white rural talent which, while largely ignored for years by the main music establishment, formed the basis for rock music. "What happened at King couldn't have happened in New York or Los Angeles," said Robert Santelli, the Rock Hall's historian and noted blues writer. "Cincinnati always had one foot in the North and one in the South, with access to blacks in the industrial cities as well as the Appalachians."[13]

The King legacy of more than 10,000 recordings in 25 years

qualifies Nathan as one of the most prolific American record producers of all time. His innovations helped steer the record industry through an exciting period, and yet he would probably say that he was only trying to earn a buck. Some original King R&B albums now fetch more than $1,000 from collectors. And hundreds of King titles have been digitally remastered and issued on CD compilations. With Nathan's "music of the little people" now a worldwide product and a legitimate part of America's musical heritage, the king of King has finally obtained long-overdue recognition.

Little Labels—Big Sound

Five / **Duke-Peacock Records**

"I had two strikes against me. I was black, and I was in the record business."

—Don Robey, owner of Duke-Peacock Records

Rock 'n' roll's first multicultural experience might have occurred in August 1952, when Willie Mae "Big Mama" Thornton, a 300-pound blues singer, ambled into a studio in southwest Los Angeles, California, to record for Don Robey, a black label owner from Houston, Texas. Band leader Johnny Otis, a Greek who lived and operated in the black world, handed to Thornton a song called "Hound Dog," a twelve-bar blues number written by teenage Jewish songwriters Jerry Leiber and Mike Stoller.

"Jerry sat in the booth; I stayed on the floor," Stoller said. "Johnny got on his drums and tuned his drums back. Jerry also said to Big Mama, 'Now I want you to growl.' She said, 'Don't be tellin' me how to sing!' But she tried it, and it worked. We got it in two takes." [1]

In early 1953, Thornton's "Hound Dog" topped the national rhythm and blues (R&B) charts and spawned a hit answer record, "Bearcat" by Rufus Thomas on Sun Records. To test the record's originality, co-publisher Robey sued for copyright infringement and won. But he didn't bother paying Leiber and Stoller, so they appointed their mothers as legal guardians and sued Robey. When he finally wrote them a check, it bounced.

Four years later, after hearing the song performed in Las Vegas, Elvis Presley recorded an up-tempo version using the original arrangement and cleaned-up lyrics. Presley's rendition topped both the R&B and pop charts, but few white listeners knew the song's origins, or that "Hound Dog" was a black slang expression referring to a man who sought a woman to take care of him — not the other way around.

Thornton's "Hound Dog" represented what rock 'n' roll would become: spontaneous, litigious, risqué. Presley's version represented rock's future multimillion-dollar industry. Though the public now identifies the song with Presley and RCA Records, Thornton's lesser-known rendition on Robey's small Peacock Records helped to spur the evolution of black R&B into rock music. His Peacock and later, Duke, labels produced an outpouring of R&B and gospel in the 1950s that influenced not only rock music, but also black soul music recorded a decade later on Berry Gordy's Motown label and other record companies.

74

Robey turned America's racial barriers to his advantage by recording R&B when it was little more than an underground phenomenon. When white radio stations ignored his records, he broke them on the few black stations operating in the South. He booked gospel singers mostly in black churches, and his blues acts in a network of black country bars and ghetto nightclubs called the Chitlin' Circuit. Robey produced records for Johnny Ace, Bobby "Blue" Bland, The Original Five Blind Boys, The Mighty Clouds of Joy, The Bells of Joy, Clarence "Gatemouth" Brown, Roy Head, O. V. Wright, Carl Carlton, and many others. Now, many decades later, their recordings appear worldwide in reissue anthologies.

Robey was a clever entrepreneur. When white artists covered his records, he collected the publishing royalties and continued to seek out other black performers whose music might also cross over into the white market. He founded successful nightclubs, a major booking agency, a record shop, song publishing companies, a pressing plant, a black beauty products company, and other non-music businesses. He taught Texas record producers how to operate independently, and demonstrated that a Southern black man could successfully lead his own music company.

From his early days, Robey learned how to cut a business deal. Born in 1903, he roamed Houston's black Fifth Ward, dropped out of high school, and gambled for a living. But after he married and became a father, he pursued legitimate enterprises, including his own profitable taxi company. Also, he helped a local music promoter bring black acts to Houston. Robey always enjoyed mingling with entertainers and the people they attracted, and he began promoting ballroom dances, boxing matches, golf tournaments, and rodeos.

In 1945, Robey opened the Bronze Peacock Dinner Club in a concrete-block building at 2809 Erastus St., in a poor Houston neighborhood flanked by factories. The club's exotic name reflected on both his light skin and dapper appearance. He wore expensive suits and diamond rings and was sometimes mistaken for white. Robey started the Peacock at the close of World War II, when Houston and the nation were eager for entertainment. The club attracted a mixed crowd, which danced to the music of Ruth Brown, Louis Jordan,

Lionel Hampton, and Aaron "T-Bone" Walker. Guests also enjoyed Robey's popular gambling room, but a robbery during business hours forced him to install gun slots and one-way mirrors and to hire a personal security force. Flanked by bodyguards, Robey paraded the club smoking thick cigars. He carried moneybags and signed eager performers on a whim.

Robey became a local music mogul at the same time Houston's black population was growing. Even before World War II, blacks sought work in the southeastern Texas city. From 1920 to 1940, its black population grew from 35,000 to 86,000. After the war, blacks migrated from East Texas, Arkansas, and Louisiana to seek jobs in Houston's factories and refineries. They settled in the city's segregated Third, Fourth, Fifth, and Sixth Wards, which supported such clubs as the Eldorado Ballroom, Club Ebony, and Club Matinee. On black radio stations KCOH and KYOK, disc jockeys broadcast shows and talent contests. In 1947, local producer Bill Quinn found bluesman Lightnin' Hopkins singing in a Dowling Street bar. His discovery led the independent labels to Houston, where they signed such bluesmen as Hopkins, Peppermint Harris, Little Willie Littlefield, Lester Williams, and Big Walter Price.

That same year, young guitarist Clarence "Gatemouth" Brown spent his last six dollars to take a taxi to Robey's Bronze Peacock. When popular singer-guitarist T-Bone Walker abruptly left the stage to nurse an aching ulcer, Brown jumped up on the stage and joined the band. The crowd loved him. Robey signed him to a management contract. Eddie Mesner, an owner of California's Aladdin Records, soon heard Brown in the Peacock and negotiated a recording deal with Robey. Aladdin recorded four sides which failed commercially. When Aladdin dropped Brown, Robey blamed insufficient promotion.

His frustration with Aladdin Records led Robey to form his own Peacock label. A Robey employee, Evelyn Johnson, recalled an exchange with the boss: "'We don't need the Mesners. We can make our own records.' I said, 'We will?' and he replied, 'Oh, yes.' I asked, 'How do you go into the record business?' and he answered, 'Hell, I don't know. That's for you to find out.' " [2] The first record, Brown's

"Didn't Reach My Goal," backed with "Atomic Energy" (Peacock 1500), was issued in late 1949.

Brown's versatility made him a solid performer on which to build a new label. The Louisiana native grew up in Texas playing banjo, fiddle, harmonica, and mandolin at local gatherings. His early blues recordings on Peacock, with driving rhythm and horns, influenced the emerging R&B sound. His association with Robey resulted in more than 50 singles through 1960, but only one release, the double-sided "Mary Is Fine" and "My Time Is Expensive" from 1949, entered *Billboard*'s national jukebox charts. Still, Brown's early recordings influenced a generation of blues players, such as Albert Collins and Johnny Copeland. Ultimately his reputation spread nationally and into Europe. (In 1997, almost 40 years after his first records with Robey, Brown received his seventh Grammy nomination for an album encompassing cajun, swing, bluegrass, blues, and more. Today, he characterizes his playing style as American music, Texas style.)

In 1952, Robey connected with three other singers who could blow the roof off any nightclub: Marie Adams, Big Mama Thornton, and Little Richard Penniman, soon known as Little Richard. Although they never sold enough records to satisfy Robey, they established the label's reputation for hard-driving R&B. That June, Adams gave Robey his first R&B hit with an up-tempo blues song, "I'm Gonna Play the Honky Tonks." Adams, a Houston homemaker, was almost as large as Thornton. Robey promoted her as "Ollie Marie Adams, blues and torch singer." When "Hound Dog" hit in 1953, the 27-year-old Thornton attracted large crowds to the Bronze Peacock. She had been on the road since age 14, when she left her minister father and church-singer mother in Alabama. After working with the Hot Harlem Revue from 1941 to 1948, she settled in Houston and toured for Robey with Little Esther and Johnny Ace in the 1950s.

Little Richard in the 1940s sang in New Orleans with the Tempo Toppers, a gospel-influenced group that included vocalists Jimmy Swam, Barry Lee Gilmore, and Robert "Billy" Brooks. Robey signed them after an audition at his Club Matinee, and they later recorded with the Johnny Otis band. In 1953, Robey released two records by the Tempo Toppers, but nothing happened, and Penniman left the label to pursue a solo career. In the mid-1950s he pioneered the rock sound on Specialty Records with "Tutti Frutti," "Long Tall Sally," and "Good Golly, Miss Molly."

Penniman claimed that Robey beat him and singer Paul Monday in Robey's office until Penniman signed a contract: "He jumped on me, knocked me down, and kicked me in the stomach. It gave me a hernia that was painful for years. I had to have an operation. He was known for beating people up, though. He would beat everybody up but Big Mama Thornton. He was scared of her. She was built like a bull." [3]

Robey, about six feet tall and weighing 250 pounds, could intimidate even his roughest performers, many of whom disagreed with him on artistic and business matters. Some Robey associates described him as a gangster and worse, but he was clearly a complex personality. His quick, violent temper contrasted with a calm, smooth exterior. Few people knew him well, and he rarely revealed private feelings. (He was once said to have lost $7,000 on a dice game without flinching.)

A sinister mythology began to swirl around him. Rumors circulated about Robey beating artists, pulling a .45-caliber pistol, and paying royalties only when he wanted. Even Clarence Brown, the first Peacock recording artist, eventually had a falling out with his boss. "As time went by it was clear my feelings for him deteriorated," Brown said. "I started out feeling like he was a father of mine." [4] Other times, Robey could be cordial with an air of refinement, which his business associates appreciated. "He was always very kind to me," said William Holford, owner of ACA Studios and engineer on many Robey records. "He was a gentleman." [5]

Some artists called Robey's company a plantation, but at the time, there were few other options for black R&B performers. Robey could find them good material, promote their records, and package their tours when most record companies wouldn't bother. "In those days," Robey said, "R&B was felt to be degrading, low, and not to be heard by respectable people."[6]

Southern black gospel, on the other hand, not only was a

Little Labels—Big Sound

growing record market, but also reached a "respectable" audience as well. By 1950, black gospel groups were receiving more radio time, even on some white Southern stations. But, as with black secular music, the major labels all but ignored gospel, giving Robey and other independents a niche. In the early 1950s, Robey signed the Jackson Harmoneers from near Jackson, Mississippi, a group later renamed the Original Five Blind Boys, featuring lead vocalist Archie Brownlee. The group ascended when Reverend Purcell Perkins joined as trainer and changed their "jubililee" singing style to hard gospel, focusing on Brownlee's soulful voice. According to music historian Arnold Shaw, Brownlee helped to originate the now-familiar scream used in soul music.

The group's third Peacock release, "Our Father," was no more than "The Lord's Prayer" spoken to drum beat with soulful reflection. The record hit the top 10 on *Billboard*'s jukebox chart and became a gospel standard. It influenced other gospel groups to add rhythm sections. Robey explained years later: " 'Our Father' and 'Peace In The Valley' by Red Foley on Decca were the first two gospel records to ever hit the jukebox. I must add that I'm the one who put the beat into religious records. I was highly criticized when I started it, but I put in the first beat — which was not a drum — and then after the public started to buy the beat, why, then I put a drum into it. Then a guitar, then a trombone. I found that the public wanted something new in religious music, and I tried it with different instruments to see which one they would take to. They did not take to the trombone, but they did take to the guitar and drumbeat, and it got to a point where, if you didn't have a beat in a religious record, you had no sales." [7]

Robey's innovative approach to gospel recording attracted performers nationwide. At one point, he had more than 100 groups under contract to Peacock. He recorded the Christland Singers and the female Golden Harps, both from Chicago, and Sister Jessie Mae Renfro (her publicity photographs said, "With Soul") from Dallas and the Reverend I. H. Gordon from New Orleans. In a 1952 trade advertisement, Robey bragged that the Bells of Joy, an Austin group, sold 26,000 copies of "Stop Right Now, It's Praying Time" before its release. The record followed the group's big hit, "Let's Talk about

Jesus," which sold several hundred thousand copies. In 1953, Robey recorded the Dixie Hummingbirds, whose most popular Peacock disc, "Let's Go Out to the Programs," implored listeners to attend gospel concerts and keep their faith burning. More groups arrived at Peacock: the Sensational Nightingales, Pilgrim Jubilee Singers, the Spirit of Memphis Quartet, the Sunset Travelers, the Gospelaires, and the Mighty Clouds of Joy, a top gospel group of the modern era.

From his roster of gospel singers, Robey found performers for his secular music. Joe Hinton came from the Spirit of Memphis Quartet; Ted Taylor, from Mighty Clouds of Joy; O. V. Wright, from the Sunset Travelers. But most Peacock religious singers stayed true to their calling and recorded long-lasting spiritual music.

While gospel music became a big part of Peacock in the early 1950s, Robey still sought a larger share of the R&B market. Seeking a merger with another R&B record company, he discovered an upstart Memphis, Tennessee, label called Duke. It was founded by David James Mattis, the white program director of black WDIA radio. The station operated only during the day, allowing Mattis to record sessions at night with performers who auditioned for radio programs. Robey felt Duke's blues roster would complement Peacock's heavy gospel roster. Unlike record producer Sam Phillips, who at the time recorded mostly known blues artists in Memphis and leased the masters to independents, Mattis recorded unknown performers and pressed the records on his small label. He bought a drafting set and designed Duke's purple and gold label logo, resembling the V front of a Cadillac. He signed young black singers Johnny Ace, Rosco Gordon, and Bobby Bland.

Robey approached Mattis about a partnership in Duke. Already preoccupied with the radio station, Mattis thought that a partnership would free him from dealing with distributors and pressing plants and allow more time for him to produce and write. But the partnership wasn't cordial for long as a feud developed. Mattis claimed that Robey owed him money, and Robey allegedly pulled his gun. Soon after, Mattis sold his share of the partnership to Robey for $10,000, much less than he thought it was worth. Years later, Robey maintained that Mattis insisted on the sale after learning the Duke label had $38,000 in the bank. "He couldn't stand that," Robey said. "He said, 'Man, I want mine out!' So he sold me his interest for $10,000 and picked up his half of the $38,000." [8]

The split suited Robey's goal to own Duke and control its artists. He closed the Bronze Peacock and remodeled the building into a record company office with a pressing plant and a room for a studio. Robey managed many of the Duke artists who helped refine the sound of traditional blues.

Ace, the young crooner, introduced a softer, romantic sound and proved that love ballads could work in the growing R&B field. His mellow vocals led the way for the modern pop-soul sound that appealed to white kids and adults. The son of a minister, John M. Alexander Jr. played piano and sang for a living in the Memphis area after serving in the Navy during World War II. He joined the Beale Streeters, a blues group that included B. B. King, Rosco Gordon, and Junior Parker. Mattis found Alexander and renamed him Johnny Ace. In less than two years under Robey's guidance, Ace won numerous national awards, including Most-Programmed Artist of 1954 by the Disc Jockeys of America and the Citation of Achievement for 1954 by BMI.

The more adulation Ace received, the more he changed. He drank heavily, pushed the accelerator of his new Oldsmobile to the floor, left his wife and two children, and pursued nightclub women who liked his recklessness and boyish face. To look older, he grew a mustache, but emotionally he remained a kid. On the road, he bought a revolver and fired it like a cap pistol. In 1954, at a Christmas Eve concert at the Houston City Auditorium, Ace teased Big Mama Thornton with the gun in a back room. She warned him to put it away, but he refused. Earlier that day, he had removed some bullets from the chamber, handed them to a young woman, and told her they would make good souvenirs if he shot himself. Hours later, the joke became his prophecy. Apparently thinking the gun wasn't loaded, he aimed at his temple and fired. For a moment, he flashed a surprised expression, then fell dead in front of his girlfriend and Thornton. When authorities arrived, they found Ace surrounded by vodka and whiskey bottles. He lay in a gray suit with $23 in his pocket and a hole in his right temple. Justice of the Peace Walter Reagan ruled that Ace killed himself while playing Russian Roulette.

At Ace's funeral in Memphis, Mattis and 5,000 mourners viewed the body. "Too many women, too much money, too much food," Mattis said. "I went down to the wake. I looked at him and thought, 'He was happier as a cheap piano player.' "[9] Ace's biggest hit, "Pledging My Love," listing Robey as a co-writer, had been released only a few days before the shooting. Hearing the ballad on the radio, women cried in the streets. The record crossed over to white radio.

While Robey stayed busy issuing Ace memorial albums, he nurtured a new star in Bobby Bland. Having arrived in Memphis at age 18 in 1947, Bland sang with the Miniatures, a gospel group, and later, the Beale Streeters. Before entering the Army in 1952, Bland made a few records for the Chess and Modern labels. After his return in 1954, he recorded for Duke. "Bobby was just another nickel-and-dime Memphis blues singer then," Mattis said. [10] His status changed in 1957 when "Farther up the Road," a Texas shuffle, topped the national R&B charts. He followed with more than 30 records on the R&B charts, including the hits "I Pity the Fool," "Turn On Your Love Light," and "That's the Way Love Is." Bland didn't write songs or play an instrument, but he devoted his energy to interpreting songs. The stylist was also a road warrior, sometimes touring 365 days a year. He sang with Junior Parker and his Blue Flames from 1957 to 1961, then went solo on the road and achieved his great success.

Probably more than any other singer, Bland benefited from a close relationship with Robey, who possibly saw a little of himself in the struggling, young Bland. Showing an uncharacteristic warm side, Robey became Bland's mentor. "I know you never heard anything pleasant about him," Bland has said of Robey, "but he had a label and he helped a lot of people. He was a businessman, and a lot of people didn't like him in certain ways, but he was okay with me."[11]

Integral to the Bland "sound," a soulful alliance of vocals, horns, and guitar, was arranger Joe Scott. As Robey's A&R man, Scott produced Bland's records and wrote arrangements that matched Bland's emotional baritone. The sound was immediately identifiable

Little Labels—Big Sound

DLP - 79

THE SOUL OF THE MAN
"BOBBY BLAND"

"PLAYGIRL" • "DEEP IN MY SOUL"
"FEVER" • "AIN'T NOBODY'S BUSINESS"
"LET'S GET TOGETHER"
"REACH RIGHT OUT"
"I CAN'T STOP"

PHOTO and COVER DESIGN R. J. SYE

*Bobby "Blue" Bland, a smooth blues stylist from Memphis, was a
big draw for Don Robey's Duke label in the 1950s and 1960s.
Despite a contentious relationship with many of his recording
artists, Robey was a mentor to Bland.*

from the combination of brass with Bland's odd squalls and moans,
and from the unmistakable honesty in his voice. As noted on a Duke
album cover, Bland "versifies, sometimes melancholic, sometimes
gutsy, sometimes morose, but always with sincerity . . . and without
elaborate musical garniture, studio or acoustic devices." [12]

By the mid-1960s, Scott and Bland peaked with such hits as
"Back in the Same Old Bag Again," "Good Time Charlie," and "I'm

83

Too Far Gone (To Turn Around Now)." Scott gently steered Bland from jump blues to gospel-blues ballads, Bland's specialty. When Scott and Bennett left Bland a few years later, Bland lost direction, musically and personally. His career suffered briefly, but he returned to the charts in 1969 with "Gotta Get to Know You" and "Rockin' in the Same Old Boat."

While Bland turned out hits for Duke, Herman "Little Junior" Parker also emerged as a star for the label. Parker, a singer and harmonica player, first recorded for the Modern label in 1952. At Phillips' Sun Records a year later, Parker recorded a top five R&B hit, "Feelin' Good," a country-blues boogie record. (He also recorded "Mystery Train" for Sun before Elvis.) Parker's Duke hits began in 1957 with "Next Time You See Me," continuing through 1962 with "Driving Wheel," "In the Dark," and "Annie Get Your Yo-Yo." In the late 1960s, Parker recorded for Mercury and other labels, and led the group Blues Consolidated. He died in 1971.

Bland and Parker made Duke a major blues label, while Peacock maintained a gospel reputation. In 1957, Robey established the Back Beat label for white and black artists with pop potential. Robey thought a subsidiary label might help change his company's gospel-blues image in the eyes of Top 40 disc jockeys. Using fancy white (and later orange) labels with a drum and sticks logo, Back Beat distinguished itself from Peacock's conservative black and silver label and Duke's bland orange label.

Robey signed several rock bands for the label, but most of them achieved only regional popularity. When he finally received his long-desired national pop hit in 1965, it came not from a long-haired rock band but from his own musical roots and backyard. Back Beat's "Treat Her Right," a number two record on *Billboard*'s pop and R&B charts, created instant demand for Roy Head and the Traits, who had recorded the song for $500 at Houston's Gold Star Studios. Inspired by Joe Tex, Head sang with a black soul feel. Since 1958, he had worked the roadhouse bars in southeast Texas, perfecting his raw sound while punching anybody who tried to shut him up. Back Beat released "Treat Her Right" while a national group of black disc jockeys met in Houston. Against Robey's advice, Head attended the

Little Labels — Big Sound

After producing successful gospel and R&B for almost 20 years, record producer Don Robey scored his first national pop hit in 1965 with a little-known, white soul singer named Roy Head. His lone hit single, "Treat Her Right," was popular with white and black listeners.

Duke-Peacock Records

convention. Robey had figured that if the disc jockeys didn't see Head, they would think he was black and might play his record.

"It all broke loose when I attended the black DJ convention," Head said. "Don Robey wouldn't let me do any TV, so nobody knew I was white. The people at the convention weren't going to let me sing. Then Joe Scott said, 'Oh, put the boy on!' I said, 'Man, I don't know, it looks awfully dark out there.' They had to push me onto the stage. But then they started playing 'Treat Her Right,' and I started doing my flip flops and dancing, and the crowd went nuts. The record became an instant hit because all the DJs heard it." [13]

After about a year, the Traits broke up, and Robey never released an album by the band. But the hit single helped to ignite, if only briefly, rural white soul music. Head even sang in black Detroit clubs during the 1960s riots and became one of a few white singers to work the black club circuit regularly. By the mid-1970s, however, the tiny white soul rebellion had all but ended, engulfed by a disco beat. By then, Head had switched to country music, which provided several hits but no musical comfort. He has since returned, happily, to his old R&B sound.

Head liked and respected Robey, despite a disagreement over publishing rights. "He was the godfather," Head said. "He had a big, old spittoon. He'd be talking to you, and suddenly you'd see him turn and spit. He'd keep talking and never miss. He carried a pistol in a holster that he strapped to his calf. He always wore sharkskin suits and he combed his hair real nice and parted it in the middle of his high forehead. Oh, he was clean. He gave me a new Cadillac and a hundred bucks and I was determined to stay with him forever. He said, 'Roy, I'll get you a new car. Just sign on this line.' So I signed six lines." [14]

Like Head, many Houston musicians had long considered 2809 Erastus the most important address in town. But Robey seemed satisfied with only a small practice studio at his Houston headquarters. He preferred to rent independent recording studios, a decision that would hamper the development of an identifiable Duke-Peacock sound in the 1960s. A decade earlier, when Robey still recorded often in Houston, he hired such talented session players as pianist

Little Labels—Big Sound

Teddy Reynolds, drummer Sonny Freeman, bassist Hamp Simmons, guitarists Clarence Hollimon, Johnny Brown, and Wayne Bennett, and trumpeter Joe Scott's tight horn section. But Robey increasingly depended on independent producers in other major cities. As a result, Robey never maintained a permanent house band, as black-music labels Stax and Motown established in the mid-1960s.

Perhaps Robey thought a commercial studio operated by a black man might not attract enough outside clients to be profitable. After all, race was an important factor in life and business in the 1950s South. He never forgot the telephone call from a white Southern distributor who immediately hung up when Robey confirmed he was a black man. "I had two strikes against me," Robey said. "I was black, and I was in the record business." [15]

In the 1960s, civil-rights activists turned the white South upside down with lawsuits, demonstrations, and sit-ins. Tempers exploded. Through the turmoil, Robey continued to sell records, mostly to black people. Ironically, the fall of segregation contributed to Robey's declining grip on the black music scene. Segregation had placed Robey's company within cultural boundaries. The growing acceptance of black music by young white listeners blurred those boundaries.

By 1970, major labels controlled much of the R&B record market, with international conglomerates owning large segments of the American record industry. By keeping overhead low and expectations high, Duke-Peacock survived while other independents failed. Also, interest was growing in Robey's vast catalog of classic blues, gospel, and R&B. No longer did his music upset "respectable" people. His records were now an integral part of the American music scene and were being used increasingly in movies, television commercials, and other pop culture outlets. Big Mama Thornton, for example, inspired a generation of 1960s rockers, including another Texas Gulf Coast singer, Janis Joplin, who recorded Thornton's "Ball and Chain." (Thornton was inducted into the Blues Foundation Hall of Fame in 1984, the year she died.)

In 1973, just before disco took hold of the record business, Robey sold Duke-Peacock, his publishing companies, and affiliated labels to ABC-Dunhill Records and agreed to serve as its consultant. His final national triumph came with Carl Carlton's remake of Robert Knight's "Everlasting Love." Surpassing the original, Carlton's ABC-Back Beat single reached the top 10 pop charts and did nearly as well in R&B in September 1974.

By then, Robey had established other priorities outside the record business. The athletic cowboy planned to work on his ranch, breed thoroughbreds, promote rodeos, and relax. He ran out of time. He died of a heart attack on June 16, 1975, at age 71. *Billboard* reported his death with a two-sentence notice on an inside page.

Today, Robey's legacy continues with reissues from MCA, owner of the Duke-Peacock masters. Appropriately, his Erastus Street office is now a church. No sign of the Duke-Peacock empire remains, but gospel songs still echo through the old neighborhood on Sunday mornings. "I probably couldn't find the building if I went over there," Head said. "It's been so long. The place is history now, man. All past." [16]

Six / **Sun Records**

"I didn't even know how to spell suede."

—Rock legend Carl Perkins

No single person is responsible for the birth of rock 'n' roll, but Sam Phillips was at least a midwife. The music genre's most important record producer in the 1950s never sang a note for his Sun Records label in Memphis, Tennessee, but he was its real star. He had a special affinity with his artists and a cultural appreciation of their songs. To Phillips, the distinctive music recorded on his little label was always more than a commodity; it was his Southern heritage.

Today, Phillips is known for discovering Elvis Presley, Jerry Lee Lewis, and Carl Perkins. So much has been written about Sun that it has become a mythical kingdom on the Mississippi River whose founder has been caught between fact, fantasy, and Elvis. One fact is certain: Sun Records in the mid-1950s pioneered a new sound with young, brash, and energetic singers who created a blend of country and rhythm and blues (R&B) known as rockabilly. What Phillips and his performers unleashed from a small studio along a working-class Memphis street reverberated across the nation and shaped the sound of rock 'n' roll.

The little Sun studio was progressive, both musically and socially. Perhaps Phillips wasn't the most meticulous producer and businessman, but he was a visionary. He pulled into orbit the region's most original and enthusiastic performers. Without his intervention into the lives of these Southern musicians, many of Sun's recording acts might have gone no farther than a neighborhood nightclub. At a time of growing social tension in the South, Phillips endured his community's taunts and disregarded the predictions: beat music was too sexual and would lead to immoral behavior, such as drug use, and race mixing. While he is lauded today as a social innovator in the music industry, Phillips was hardly considered so when he was making records more than 40 years ago. But because his recording studio celebrated both the white and black elements of Southern music, Samuel Cornelius Phillips will always be remembered.

The youngest of a tenant farmer's eight children, Phillips was born January 5, 1923, near Florence, Alabama, an area rich in country, gospel, and blues music. In high school, Phillips conducted the school band. His onstage presence so impressed the manager of local WLAY radio, that he was hired as a part-time announcer. After his father died at the beginning of World War II, Phillips quit school and took a job in a funeral parlor, where he faced the unenviable task of consoling bereaved families. The job taught Phillips how to handle people tactfully in emotional situations, a skill that served him well later.

However, the radio business was in his blood. At night, he studied sound engineering at Alabama Polytechnical Institute, and eventually he found radio jobs in Alabama and Tennessee. At WREC in Memphis in the mid-1940s, he gained experience, earned a decent living, and fulfilled a dream of living in the "City of the Blues." It had always seemed a majestic place to him, geographically and musically. While spinning jazz, blues, and pop records on a Saturday show, he became fascinated by the many small, independent labels that crossed his desk.

His passion for audio technology prompted an interest in how these records were made and led him in late 1949 to create the Memphis Recording Service. Phillips was now raising a family, so he kept his radio job, but a friend lent him money to buy recording equipment and rent a vacant storefront at 706 Union Avenue near downtown. In January 1950, he opened the doors and handed out business cards that read: "We record anything—anywhere—anytime." Transcriptions, commercials, weddings, vanity records: he did them all.

Phillips opened for business at a time when Memphis had developed into a regional economic center. It had long been a top cotton market, and the city's agricultural companies also traded in sugar cane, hay, corn, sweet potatoes, and other crops. The post–World War II boom had resulted in the addition of the manufacturing of chemicals, machinery, rubber products, and furniture. From 1940 to 1950, as rural people migrated to the city seeking better-paying factory jobs, the population grew from about 293,000 to 396,000.

Memphis also had a vibrant African-American culture, with a musical history steeped in black country blues from the nearby Mississippi Delta. Along Beale Street, the black community had its own 2,000-seat auditorium, Church's Park, as well as black dentists, doctors, grocers, tailors, undertakers, and other business people. When Phillips opened his small recording studio, Beale was the black community's Main Street, and he was drawn to its rhythms. After World War II, the city's black music scene blossomed from an expanding radio market. WDIA, a popular white-managed station, played black music. Dewey Phillips, the white host of WHBQ's R&B show, "Red, Hot and Blue," introduced black music to young whites. By 1949, Memphis also had a record-pressing plant, Plastic Products, and a record distributor called Music Sales. They became the foundation of a local record industry.

In the early 1950s, Phillips recorded local blues singers and leased the masters to labels across the country. His recording method was simple: cut a song several times and keep the version with the most feeling. He recorded B. B. King, a local singer, guitarist, and disc jockey, and Joe Hill Louis for the RPM label, as well as Rosco Gordon, Howlin' Wolf, and Jackie Brenston for Chicago's Chess, the leading blues label. Brenston's "Rocket 88," a song about an Olds-mobile featuring Ike Turner on piano, topped the national R&B charts in June 1951. A forerunner of the rock 'n' roll record, it was the first of three top ten R&B hits that Phillips produced in the early 1950s.

Despite the national exposure, Phillips earned barely enough money to pay the bills. Pressured into action, he quit the radio station to concentrate solely on his recording activities. He boldly told Chess Records, the major outlet for his masters, that he needed more money. Phillips also began to face competition for local talent. By 1952, Chess, Modern, and other labels had already signed Memphis performers, and a new local label, Duke, actively recorded and promoted local singers as well. In order to survive, Phillips decided to sell records through his own label.

"I truly did not want to open a record label," he said, "but I was forced into it by those labels either coming to Memphis to record or taking my artists elsewhere. Sun Records was forced on me, but at the same time, it presented the opportunity to do exactly as I wanted." [1]

Little Labels — Big Sound

Phillips sketched a rough logo of a rooster crowing beneath a big sun and asked a local artist to design a brown and yellow label. He named his record company after the sun because he believed it was the universal power. Phillips issued the first Sun release in March 1952: "Drivin' Slow," by a 16-year-old black alto saxophone player named Johnny London. In the studio, Phillips had suspended a rectangular object over London which created the effect of someone playing a saxophone in a long hallway. When the 78-rpm discs arrived later that month from the Memphis pressing plant, Phillips proudly mounted one on the studio wall. Sun Record 175 became his symbol of independence. The teenage saxophonist's first recording never sold beyond the region, but it allowed Phillips to merge his dual interests, the recording studio and the label, to produce a sound based on gut feeling.

An unlikely camaraderie existed between the black performers and this white Southern studio owner, but Phillips was not just any man. He was strong-willed, charismatic, and opinionated. He swayed performers with his dark, penetrating eyes and intelligence. Despite segregation and growing racial tension in several Southern cities, black and white relations were often cordial on a personal level, especially among the poor. They shared common problems and a culture of hard work. Their music often intersected in the fields. When Phillips, a tenant farmer's son, talked to poor blues and hillbilly singers, they spoke a common language. He defied the segregationists by associating with blacks and, worse, by openly promoting and enjoying their music. Phillips didn't care what his neighbors thought.

"I didn't have to look it up to know B.B. King was talented," Phillips said. "And I knew what I wanted. I wanted something *ugly*. Ugly and honest. I knew that these people were disenfranchised. They were politically disenfranchised and economically disenfranchised, and, to tell the truth, they were musically disenfranchised." [2]

In the early 1950s, Phillips recorded modest hits by Rufus Thomas, a singer and disc jockey, and Little Junior Parker, composer of "Mystery Train" and other songs who later moved to the Duke

93

label. Sun also featured the Prisonaires, five inmates from Nashville's Tennessee State Penitentiary, who received special permission to travel to Memphis to record.

But Sun wasn't limited to R&B music. Phillips auditioned anybody who walked into his office. This policy encouraged a parade of characters who sought recording deals with Sun, including a balding country singer in his thirties named Malcolm Yelvington. A native of Covington, Tennessee, Yelvington moved to Memphis to become a welder. At night, he sang country music. His name, age, looks, and growing family at home didn't make him star material, but he persisted. In late 1953, he walked into the Sun office and told Phillips, "I hear you're looking for singers."

"Well, what kind of music do you do?" Phillips asked.

"Country," Yelvington responded.

"I'm not really interested in country right now."

"Well, what kind of music do you want to hear?"

"I don't know. And I won't know until I hear it." [3]

In 1954, Phillips reluctantly agreed to find suitable material for the personable singer. At the time, however, Phillips was experimenting with a 19-year-old Elvis Presley, a local truck driver, and developing the underpinnings of rockabilly in Memphis. The blues had set Phillips on the path of seeking white musicians who rocked with a black beat. Thus, he gradually lost interest in Yelvington until his band, the Star Rhythm Boys, jammed on an R&B song, "Drinkin' Wine Spodee-O-Dee," in the Sun studio. Phillips released it as Sun 211.

As Yelvington recalled: "A woman from the front office at the plant called me in and said, 'Malcolm, did you hear your record on the radio?' I said, 'My record?' I didn't even know it was out. So me and the band took off to promote it in Arkansas and Tennessee, where it was getting some air play. The record eventually sold 6,000 to 8,000 copies, but it was not really a hit. I can't blame Sun Records and Sam Phillips. The label had Elvis then. I just happened to be number two. They didn't call me Pop, but they could have. The companies all seemed to be looking for good looks, hair, youth. And I didn't have any."

Little Labels—Big Sound

Yelvington kept his day job while other unknown rockabilly singers took his place in the Sun studio: Warren Smith, Billy Lee Riley, Barbara Pittman, Sonny Burgess, Charlie Feathers, Glenn Honeycutt, and, of course, Presley, Sun's prized rookie who turned local teenagers into screaming anxiety cases, but who could not yet produce hit records. Many of Presley's rockabilly contemporaries in Memphis have long been forgotten. While the contributions of Sun's Presley, Lewis, and Perkins are well documented, the music of Burgess, Riley, and Phillips' other rockabilly acts collectively helped to mold the new sound in small nightclubs across the South and create a hybrid alternative to the black R&B that was also attracting young listeners.

Presley's rise, on the other hand, has been retold countless times, the way religious experiences are retold to reinforce the faith. He walked into the Sun studio to record an acetate, possibly for his mother or maybe for himself. Upon hearing this untrained but unusual talent, Phillips nurtured the kid for months. Other producers might have changed Presley's style, a fascinating blend of white and black influences, but Phillips let him and other Sun singers pursue their own musical routes. Presley's feel was for country with a beat, fresh and raw. Phillips teamed him with bassist Bill Black and guitarist Scotty Moore, skilled professionals whose studio playing mirrored their stage performances. "I called Scotty Moore, told him to get Bill Black and come in and work with Presley," Phillips said. "I told him: 'I've got a young man and he's different. He's nervous and timid and extremely polite. Work with him and see what you can do.' It took us a while. We worked on and off for six months. There were a lot of songs we could have cut, but they weren't different. It was up to me to see the uniqueness of his talent, and to go, hopefully, in the right direction with it." [4]

Presley's first Sun record, cut in 1954, was a classic blend of white and black influences: Arthur Crudup's R&B tune "That's All Right Mama," with Bill Monroe's bluegrass tune, "Blue Moon of Kentucky," on the flip side. By 1955, Presley was billed locally as the "King of Western Bop," and Phillips released new singles of Presley singing "Good Rockin' Tonight" (a hit in 1948 for Wynonie Harris on

King), "Milkcow Blues," "Baby Let's Play House," and "Mystery Train." The shy, polite Presley suddenly became a sensation with kids across the South.

Like Presley, most singers on Sun had never recorded before. Nevertheless, Phillips let them do what came naturally. As music writer Rich Kienzle observed, Phillips found ways to make the performers' rough edges work for them. His musicians were the antithesis of Nashville's slick country-pop session players. They were roadhouse boys who hungered for money and recognition. So Phillips handpicked his best performers, published their songs through his new BMI publishing firms, Hi Lo and Fort Knox, and helped them evolve into the Sun house band.

Phillips refined the studio band concept. His early group, including steel guitar player Stan Kesler (later the producer of Sam the Sham and the Pharaohs) and popular local bassist Marcus Van Story, played country music. By the mid-1950s, however, Phillips assembled a rockabilly studio band that included much of Billy Lee Riley's rocking band. Other players floated into the studio as Phillips sought the right sound. Operating a house band required patience, an ear for talented musicians, and time to experiment with them.

"Sam didn't have a clock in the studio," said Johnny Cash. "He didn't let me feel like I was spending anybody's money by just singing new songs. After an hour or two, he'd say, 'OK, what else you got? Let's keep going till we get your best.' I loved that in a producer. That's what Sam did with all of us at Sun; he tried to find the uniqueness in each of us. He didn't try to simply make us sound like everyone else." [5]

Perhaps Phillips' greatest strength was his flexibility, which allowed the Sun performers to pioneer the new rockabilly sound. "I tried to play like Bill Monroe," Sun artist Charlie Feathers said. "A lot of bluegrass is done fast. Years ago, people had the upright bass and fiddle around the house. They'd start poppin' that old bass. All they done down here was that poppin'. Catgut strings had a unique sound. Gave plenty of bottom. Then somebody put cotton-patch blues with bluegrass and created rockabilly. Most beautiful music I ever heard in my life. Sun didn't have a studio suited to country. I think we got

Little Labels — Big Sound

it goin' down here, man, 'cause we had the accent. But what really made those early records was slapback echo, the slappin' bass, and no drums. What a sound! Right off the floor and onto the record." [6]

While Sun Records in 1955 produced a raucous new sound, Phillips learned that talent alone didn't create hit records. He needed operating capital. So he offered Presley's contract for $35,000, an unprecedented amount for a performer with primarily regional appeal. Columbia's Mitch Miller offered $20,000 and Atlantic's Ahmet Ertegun $25,000. Then Phillips hesitated. He sought the opinion of Kemmons Wilson, a friend and successful Memphis homebuilder. Phillips respected Wilson, builder in 1952 of Memphis' new Holiday Inn motel. (Just as Phillips believed American roots music would attract a national audience, Wilson knew the proposed national interstate highway system would change the way people travel, and a chain of quality motels could make a fortune. By 1968, he had built more than 1,000 Holiday Inns.) After speaking with Wilson, Phillips in late 1955 sold Presley's contract to RCA for the $35,000 he originally sought. He invested the money in his Sun operations and the Holiday Inn chain. From that seed money, he eventually became a millionaire, buying studios and radio stations.

But in early 1956, Phillips also used some of the capital to promote his growing roster of young singers, including Carl Perkins. A founding father of rockabilly, Perkins worked for the Colonial Bakery in Jackson, Tennessee, and sang in local beer joints. In 1954, he heard one of Presley's Sun records on the radio. The rockabilly feel was familiar to Perkins, who had been doing it, too. Perkins, who cites Hank Williams as a primary influence, defines rockabilly as a marriage of the white man's lyrics and the black man's soul. As a sharecropper's son in northwest Tennessee, Perkins had heard plenty of black music as a boy in the 1940s, and he blended the black and white musical styles. Perkins assumed that Phillips would be interested in his music, so he traveled to Memphis and asked to cut a record. Phillips put Perkins on his new Flip label, to sing country. Not much happened, initially, but everything changed when Perkins wrote "Blue Suede Shoes" to showcase his rockabilly sound.

The song's origin is murky. Perkins' friend and fellow Sun artist,

Johnny Cash, has claimed that he gave Perkins the idea based on an incident that occurred while Cash was in the Army. Perkins remembered it differently: "I heard a boy tell a girl one time, 'Now, don't you step on my suedes.' It happened right here in Jackson in a club. It bothered me because she was a beautiful girl. I looked down, and she had stepped on them, and she was embarrassed and hurt. I thought, man, I don't own a pair of suede shoes, but if I did, I'd kick them jewels off, and I'd give them to her. That bothered me so much that I could not go to sleep that night. I was living in a government housing project. I was up at 3 o'clock in the morning. The song had to be born that night. I kept thinking, Don't step on my blue suede shoes. Then I thought of that old nursery rhyme: one for the money, two for the show, three to get ready, four to go. That's the way it got started. I couldn't find any paper to write on. We had two small babies at the time. I guess I didn't have any need for writing paper because all my people lived around here. So I took three Irish potatoes out of a brown paper bag and wrote: 'Don't step on my blue swade shoes.' I didn't even know how to spell suede." [7]

The next day, Perkins called Phillips from an elderly neighbor's house.

Phillips responded, " 'Blue Suede Shoes'? Is that like 'Oh, Dem Golden Slippers?'"

"No, no, no," Perkins said. "This is about a cat who don't want nobody stepping on his shoes."

Perkins sang his song over the phone: "One for the money, two for the show. . . ." The old man who had loaned his telephone stared at Perkins, but Phillips liked what he heard on the other end.

In January 1956, Phillips released "Blue Suede Shoes," backed with "Honey, Don't," another Perkins original. Phillips pushed the record into the national arena. Good reviews brought air play, and by April, Perkins topped the R&B and country charts. Only Presley's "Heartbreak Hotel" on RCA, another rockabilly record, prevented Perkins from topping the *Billboard*'s national pop charts. The hit prompted an invitation to appear on NBC's Perry Como Show. While driving to New York City on March 22, 1956, Dick Stuart, Perkins' manager, fell asleep at the wheel and hit a truck in Dela-

Little Labels—Big Sound

A *pioneer of the mid-1950s rockabilly sound, Carl Perkins first sang his song "Blue Suede Shoes" over the telephone to Sam Phillips, owner of Sun Records. The recording became a hit for Sun in 1956.*

ware. The truck driver was killed. Perkins' brothers, Jay and Clayton, were seriously injured, and Jay eventually died. Carl suffered a cracked skull and broken shoulder. While he was healing in Tennessee, radio stations worldwide played his record, which eventually sold a million copies. "Blue Suede Shoes" best represents the essence of rockabilly: sparse, bright, rhythmic. One of rock's most influential records, it has become a rockabilly legacy. It thrust Sun into the national pop arena.

Using the record's profits, Phillips aggressively signed and promoted more artists on the Sun label. Among the most flamboyant and talented was Jerry Lee Lewis, the singer-pianist from Louisiana whose series of hits for Sun included "Great Balls of Fire" and "Whole Lotta Shakin' Goin' On." As the studio engineer, Phillips contributed to Lewis' sound by using "slapback," the distinctive tape-delay effect heard on "Great Balls of Fire" and many other Sun records. It provided an explosive sound that complemented frenzied rockabilly vocals. Another Sun artist, Johnny Cash, made in-roads with "I Walk the Line" in 1956. (Phillips eventually packaged a tour with Lewis, Cash, and Perkins.) Other Sun acts included Roy Orbison, whose "Rockhouse" and "Ooby Dooby" drew attention but few sales, and singer/songwriter Charlie Rich, later dubbed "The Silver Fox," a smooth singer who found commercial success in country music in the 1970s. Meanwhile, Perkins recorded "Boppin' the Blues," "Dixie Fried," and other fine songs, but none matched the sales of "Blue Suede Shoes."

At the same time, Phillips recorded many now-obscure singers who packed the clubs around Memphis. Rockabilly fever spread. "The crowds used to go wild," recalled bassist Van Story, who toured with Perkins and other artists. "The reaction was unbelievable—people wiggling, jumping, dancing. One night we warned Carl that he'd better watch out for the crowds, because they were particularly eager. If they ever got a hold of you, well, they'd tear your clothes off. Well, out on stage goes old Carl, getting a little too close to the edge. The first thing you know, he's standing there in his pants. They ripped his jacket and shirt off." [8]

Van Story played "bull fiddle," as he called the upright bass, for

Little Labels—Big Sound

Jerry Lee Lewis followed Elvis Presley and Carl Perkins into the Sun Records studio in Memphis and recorded a series of smash hits.

Warren Smith, who recorded "Ubangi Stomp" and Cash's "Rock 'n' Roll Ruby" in 1956. Unlike many Sun performers, Smith, from Humphreys County, Mississippi, recorded both country and rockabilly. Though "Ubangi Stomp" failed nationally, the novelty song has been kept alive by rockabilly bands ever since. In the 1950s, listeners considered the song cute; today, it would likely be seen as racist. During Smith's performance of the song, Van Story would hang a little shrunken head on his bass, though the Ubangi tribes had nothing to do with head shrinking. Rockabilly fans also enjoy Smith's "Miss Froggie," another novelty song remembered mostly for guitarist Al Hobson's fierce picking.

Among Phillips' rockabilly singers, Billy Lee Riley, from Pocahontas, Arkansas, may have rocked the hardest. Riley and his band, the "Little Green Men," recorded such unusual songs as "Flying Saucers Rock 'n' Roll" and "Red Hot," but they never produced a national hit. "My band was the Sun sound," Riley claimed. "We've never gotten credit for that, but it's a fact. I was doing what Elvis was doing before Elvis did it: mixing blues and hillbilly, putting a laid-back, funky beat to hillbilly music." [9]

His guitarist, Roland Janes, considered Riley one of the era's great talents, capable of anything, on and off the stage. "He could be classified as an Indian on the warpath," Janes said. [10] In retrospect, it's a wonder his recordings sounded coherent. "I think Roland is the only one [in the band] who didn't drink," Riley said. "But man, we used to come into that studio with Thunderbird wine and beer or whatever, and, before the session was over, we would all be bombed. I remember some sessions when I couldn't get out of the chair." [11]

Riley's raspy voice sounded as if he had been shouting and smoking all day. On stage, his gyrations excited the crowds. With Sun from 1956 to 1959, Riley was overshadowed by Perkins, Lewis, or whomever Phillips tried to make a star. Frustrated and angry, Riley left for Los Angeles. For years, he recorded a hodgepodge of material and styles, including a harmonica album of Beatles songs. Destined to be only a cult figure among the rockabilly faithful, he thinks Phillips neglected him. "The thing that I did was contribute," Riley said. "I didn't get credit for it." [12]

Another colorful Sun performer, Albert "Sonny" Burgess, of Newport, Arkansas, sang in the R&B style with a country repertoire. Merging the two styles in 1956, he wrote and recorded "We Wanna Boogie" and other rockabilly songs. He dyed his hair red to match his Fender Stratocaster and suit. On stage, he and his band performed a song called "The Bug," and people danced as if they were scratching bug bites. "In those days, we didn't know how to record," he said.

Little Labels—Big Sound

"Nobody ever told us what to do. We just played as if we were playing for a crowd. We thought we were big stars then, but we were really known only in our home areas. Back then, you could go up to Elvis or anybody else and just talk. The crowds really got into the music. We provided it. Now, after we're all past the prime of our lives, we're getting some attention. We may never have been big stars, but we made a little money and had a good time." [13]

Though Sun was essentially a male domain, a couple of Southern women became part of Phillips' rockabilly scene. Jean Chapel, a blonde singer and guitarist from Kentucky, recorded "Won't Be Rockin' Tonight" for Sun in 1955, before Phillips sold her contract to RCA. (During the same period, Phillips sold Presley's contract to RCA.) Billed as "The Female Elvis Presley" by RCA, she performed in flashy outfits for Alan Freed's pioneering rock 'n' roll show at the Brooklyn Paramount Theater, but she never hit the charts and soon resented the bogus "Female Elvis" billing. Eventually, she gave up the nightclub circuit to raise a child. A few years later, she began writing hit songs in Nashville for other performers.

The buxom Barbara Pittman, a childhood friend of Presley in Memphis, first recorded for Sun in 1956 after working clubs as a teenager. "We cut 'I Need a Man' in '56," she said. "I bought a copy. My mother bought a copy. Seriously, it didn't do much." [14] Phillips released eight sides for Pittman, although she felt that he never promoted her. She viewed the Sun studio as strictly a man's world. "You see, I was always a well-endowed girl, and the guys used to tell me that they didn't know how to fit a 42 into a 33–1/3 [rpm album]. By 1957, I had been taken off Sun and put on Sam's other label, Phillips International. He asked me which label I preferred, and I said I'd rather be on Phillips because it looked prettier." Eventually, Pittman moved to California, sang in clubs, and appeared in motorcycle films.

By 1960, the Sun label and its rockabilly sound was fading fast. Its major acts had moved to bigger labels, and Phillips was increasingly involved in new studios in Memphis and Nashville. (He had closed his original studio at 706 Union Avenue in 1959.) Lewis had descended into a valley of bad publicity after marrying his 13-year-

103

old cousin, and Cash signed with Columbia and recorded "The Ring of Fire" and other hits. Perkins also signed with Columbia but couldn't duplicate Cash's success.

Sun's rockabilly records greatly influenced the English rock artists of the early 1960s, especially the Beatles, only to be nearly forgotten in America for many years. When the Beatles recorded Perkins' "Honey Don't" and "Matchbox" in the mid-1960s, many American kids didn't know these songs had been created in America a decade before. However, the Beatles, especially George Harrison, has consistently praised rockabilly pioneers like Perkins and continues to call attention to the early Sun records.

During the Beatles era, the Sun operation was gradually dismantled. In 1969, Phillips sold the label to Shelby S. Singleton, a Nashville independent producer and label owner who revived Sun with several moderate hits. Essentially, Singleton operated Sun as a reissues album label, which sold briskly by mail order. With Presley's death in 1977, the Sun legacy assumed greater historical significance. Colin Escott of Canada and Martin Hawkins of England began cataloging Sun's masters and interviewing its former artists. They wrote a brief but detailed history and discography, *Catalyst: The Sun Records Story*. Without their important work, discography and anecdotal details might have been lost forever.

In the 1980s, rockabilly's pared-down sound enjoyed a revival, with bands such as the Stray Cats. Later that decade, Singleton increased production of Sun reissues. Meanwhile, Burgess, Van Story, and other Memphis rockabilly alumni formed The Original Sun Rhythm Section, which performed at the Smithsonian Institute in Washington D.C., and in Europe and recorded a compact disc for the Flying Fish label. Other old Sun rockabilly acts, including Riley, Yelvington, and Hayden Thompson, embarked on European tours in hopes of restarting their careers, but they enjoyed only a limited cult following.

After he sold the Sun label, Phillips didn't seriously consider recording again. His time had passed, and he knew it. He has remained busy overseeing varied business interests in Memphis. In 1995, he loaned to the Rock and Roll Hall of Fame and Museum

Little Labels—Big Sound

numerous Sun Records artifacts and the equipment with which he had recorded the classic hits. The Hall used his original RCA 70-D mixing board and one-track Ampex 350 tape deck to recreate the control room at Union Avenue. It was the first time that the equipment had ever been displayed. Phillips said he wanted the average person to be able to see it and appreciate what he had accomplished with hard work. Meanwhile, the original Sun studio at 706 Union Avenue in Memphis has become a cultural landmark and tourist attraction.

"People are going to wonder how we got the sound we did out of the equipment we had," Phillips said. "But you can overcome a lot of things with just a little pioneering spirit. I hope the exhibit inspires some young person to go for broke. I hope they look at it and say, 'Man, it started from this? There's hope for me.' " [15]

Seven / **Riverside Records**

"I ruined a perfectly good hobby by making it my profession."

—Riverside's Orrin Keepnews

Orrin Keepnews remembers vividly the night in 1959 when he first saw guitarist Wes Montgomery in a bar in Indianapolis, Indiana. The co-owner of Riverside Records, Keepnews had flown in from Manhattan, rented a car, and pulled up to the Turf Bar, a 50-seat club near downtown. He took a seat near the tiny stage. "I was very close to Wes, and his thumb was blurring before my eyes," Keepnews recalled. "The feeling was one of total incredulity. I had to call someone to share the moment, to establish contact with reality, so I got my wife on a pay phone and told her, 'I don't believe what I'm hearing here!' It was one of the most amazing nights of my life." [1]

Just a few weeks earlier, saxophonist Cannonball Adderly had experienced a similar amazement. He was touring through Indianapolis and heard the 35-year-old guitarist in a black, after-hours club called the Missile Room. Adderly tried to contact Keepnews immediately, but the club didn't have a telephone, and the gas station across the street was closed. Though Montgomery was barely known outside his hometown in Indiana, Adderly soon stormed into Keepnews' office in Manhattan and demanded, "We've got to have that guy on our label." [2]

Keepnews heeded the advice. In the early morning hours at the Turf Bar, Montgomery signed a contract with Riverside, a small Manhattan jazz label created in 1952 by Keepnews and Bill Grauer. By this time, Riverside had recorded many pacesetters of modern jazz: Thelonius Monk, Bill Evans, Clark Terry, Johnny Griffin, Sonny Rollins, Art Blakey, Max Roach, John Coltrane, and Nat and Cannonball Adderly. Like Montgomery, most were articulate, skilled black musicians with original approaches to playing jazz. Montgomery was a perfect fit.

Montgomery's string of straight-ahead jazz albums between 1959 and 1963 on Riverside sold several thousand copies apiece. He obtained a wider audience a few years later with pop-oriented albums on the larger Verve label. But during four years at Riverside, which went out of business in 1964, Montgomery's thumb-picking technique and melodies, which he played in octaves, defined modern jazz guitar playing. His 28 recording sessions for Riverside captured memorable moments from a career cut short by his death in 1968 at age 43.

Montgomery's experience at Riverside was commonplace. Keepnews found great jazz soloists and composers, showcased them with the best sidemen available, and recorded them prolifically. Some moved on to larger labels and greater exposure. But Keepnews capitalized on their years with Riverside and produced an enormous body of influential jazz. Years later, as an executive for the Milestone and Fantasy jazz labels, Keepnews meticulously repackaged the Riverside masters and outtakes on comprehensive reissue anthologies, which provided invaluable resource material for the young players leading the 1990s bebop resurgence.

Riverside reflected Keepnews' basic love for jazz. Before becoming a record producer, he was a serious listener of traditional jazz, a record collector, and a moonlighting jazz journalist who understood the music's evolution. "I ruined a perfectly good hobby by making it my profession," said Keepnews, who has produced jazz for four decades. "Like other jazz record producers for small labels at the time [1950s], I was a jazz fan who basically decided that I would be a jazz record producer and that was it."

As Riverside co-owner and hands-on artistic director, he scouted smoky nightclubs for promising musicians, lined up sidemen, oversaw studio and live sessions, and wrote or edited the album liner notes. Recording jazz was a very personal endeavor, and many of his favorite moments at Riverside came through his friendships with the musicians.

Keepnews attributes the birth of Riverside, and his career as a record producer, to a series of coincidences. He was born in 1923 in Manhattan, where he pursued an English degree at Columbia College and wrote jazz reviews for the college newspaper in the early 1940s. He used the free press passes to attend weekend Dixieland jazz concerts at Town Hall or to visit Max Gordon's newly created Manhattan jazz club, the soon-legendary Village Vanguard. Gordon befriended the college journalist who frequented the club to interview musicians. In 1943, before completing his degree, Keepnews entered the Army Air Corps as a navigator and radio operator on a

B–29. While stationed in Guam during World War II, Keepnews flew in bombing runs over Japan. When the war ended, he moved back to his parents' apartment in Manhattan near the college. He briefly attended graduate school, and then joined the publishing house of Simon & Schuster as an editor.

In 1948, a former college acquaintance, Bill Grauer, purchased *The Record Changer*, an eight-year-old record collector's magazine operating out of a lower Harlem storefront. Serving a niche audience of mainly enthusiasts for 1920s jazz, the magazine survived by selling classified advertisements and by often running stories contributed by the magazine's readers. Grauer asked Keepnews to be managing editor, which entailed writing and editing stories. "It gradually began to consume me, though it was essentially a non-paying sideline," Keepnews said. "Bill Grauer could be a very persuasive guy." To fill *The Record Changer*, Keepnews interviewed and profiled several leading Dixieland-style jazz players based in Manhattan, including Pee Wee Russell and Joe Sullivan.

Two of Keepnews' writing projects for *The Record Changer* influenced the direction of his life. In the late 1940s, Alfred Lion, head of New York's leading jazz independent label, Blue Note, invited Keepnews to profile Thelonius Monk for the magazine. At the time, Keepnews had been a committed jazz traditionalist and less familiar with the new jazz (bebop) movement spearheaded by Monk, Charlie Parker, Dizzy Gillespie, and others in New York. Monk responded to Keepnews' persistent questions with one-word mumbles in Lion's living room. But in writing the article, Keepnews re-evaluated the odd-sounding dissonance and rhythms that Monk was bringing to modern jazz. *The Changer* published one of the first articles on Monk, among the most gifted and idiosyncratic jazz pianists and composers. Keepnews had begun to view the modern jazz movement unfolding in his city in a different light.

The other writing project led to a business deal. In 1951, Keepnews exposed RCA Victor Records' pressing of bootleg records. He reported that RCA's production plant, which also custom-pressed discs for other companies, was pressing album compilations for a fly-by-night label, Jolly Roger Records, which had been pirating its material from old Victor and Columbia 78-rpms. RCA Victor, a vocal opponent of bootleg recordings, said it was unaware of the origins of Jolly Roger's masters. After the stories were published, RCA Victor executives started talking to Keepnews. Eventually, RCA offered to lease its old jazz master records to Keepnews and Grauer for reissue. "We looked at each other and figured, why the hell not?" Keepnews said. The partners quickly formed their own record label, Riverside, named after the telephone exchange at the magazine office. In addition to RCA Victor material, Keepnews and Grauer pursued rights to old 78-rpm jazz discs from other labels.

They soon learned a valuable lesson when RCA altered the plans. "There are certain eternal truths when dealing with a major record label (such as RCA Victor)," Keepnews said. "One is that nothing is final until everything has been signed." Instead of leasing its old records directly to Riverside, RCA wanted Keepnews and Grauer to reissue the recordings on a new RCA Victor subsidiary called Label X. It wasn't what they had in mind, but they agreed. "Still, we had already moved forward on creating our own label, so we pursued Riverside," said Keepnews. Grauer managed the finances; Keepnews managed the music end.

In 1952, they obtained rights to the 1920s Paramount blues and jazz material from record collector John Steiner, who had bought the Paramount property in the 1940s. Shortly after Grauer struck the deal, Atlantic Records, seeking to increase its presence in jazz recording, offered to pay $5,000 to Riverside to transfer the Paramount deal to Atlantic. "It would have been a piece of change, but we decided to try it ourselves," Keepnews said. Then, New York talent scout John Hammond provided access to his collection of mint-condition jazz and blues on original Paramount 78-rpm discs, including one of only two known copies of pianist Meade Lux Lewis's "Honky Tonk Train." More material was obtained when the Gennett family in Richmond, Indiana, offered old Gennett 78-rpm discs for sale. Grauer struck a deal. Thus, by 1953, the fledgling Riverside label produced 10-inch albums featuring the best 1920s jazz and blues musicians, including King Oliver, Louis Armstrong, Johnny Dodds, Jelly Roll Morton, and Ma Rainey. Grauer also arranged to

Little Labels—Big Sound

provide Riverside's master tapes of classic jazz to English Decca, which issued the London label.

In the mid-1950s, Keepnews steered Riverside in a new direction. He first produced sessions for white studio jazz musicians, including keyboard player Dick Hyman. Then, Riverside issued a trio album anchored by black bebop pianist and composer Randy Weston, a Monk disciple. In 1955, jazz writer Nat Hentoff contacted Keepnews about Monk, then 38 years old, whose career was faltering. A narcotics conviction in 1951 prevented him from obtaining the "cabaret card" required to play in New York's nightclubs. He had switched from Blue Note to the Prestige label, and his records were selling poorly, despite his stature among New York's bebop musicians.

After hearing about Monk's availability, Keepnews and Grauer never blinked. "It was a very deliberate decision to get Monk released from his Prestige contract," Keepnews said. "Monk was terribly unhappy with Prestige. We figured that, if nothing else, signing Monk would send a clear message to the industry that we were serious about modern jazz at Riverside." They paid Prestige the remaining $108.27 balance on a cash advance to Monk. When they met with him, he recalled with pleasure his profile in *The Record Changer*. (In 1956, Grauer sold the magazine due to the demands of their new record label.)

Despite his growing savvy in the jazz business, Keepnews was challenged by Monk. Keepnews found him to be an "erratic, stubborn, basically intolerant, and overwhelmingly talented artist." [3] During six years at Riverside, Monk was rarely satisfied with his recorded efforts, demanded numerous retakes in the studio, and occasionally argued with session players who struggled to play his complex arrangements. But in demanding perfection, he took jazz to a higher level. As organizer of these projects, Keepnews fostered Monk's creativity during tightly scheduled sessions and recorded enough material for several outstanding albums.

Monk's Riverside releases were among his most exploratory. To Keepnews' credit, he produced the pianist playing original songs and jazz standards in many formats: as solo pianist, with small groups, in

Though always a challenge to record, pianist and composer Thelonius Monk produced some of his most original albums in the 1950s with producer Orrin Keepnews at Riverside Records.

live club sessions, even in a live concert hall session with a six-piece horn section. Keepnews gave Monk his choice of sidemen, among them such saxophone giants as Coleman Hawkins, Sonny Rollins, Johnny Griffin, and John Coltrane. Monk's string of Riverside al-

Little Labels—Big Sound

bums in the late 1950s coincided with his return to live playing and his career blossomed, leading to a more lucrative contract with Columbia in the early 1960s. "Of my projects at Riverside, I am probably most proud of what I could help Monk to achieve," Keepnews said.

The relationship was mutually beneficial, however. By signing Monk, Keepnews tapped into a circle of great New York jazz musicians who became Riverside regulars. "Monk led me to Johnny Griffin and Coltrane and Clark Terry," Keepnews explained. "Then, Clark Terry led me to Nat and Cannonball Adderly, and they told me about Wes Montgomery. It was an important chain reaction for me. Also, they enjoyed playing with many of the same people, such as Ark Blakey or Wynton Kelly, who were also with Riverside. It made us feel like a repertory company; the label had a distinct sound."

For Monk's first two albums at Riverside, Keepnews selected recognizable standards in a trio setting, with sessions at Rudy Van Gelder's studio in Hackensack, New Jersey. (The studio, site of countless jazz records for Blue Note and others, was Gelder's living room.) For the first album, a Duke Ellington tribute, Monk arrived at the studio, sat down at the piano, and ran through the songs as if rehearsing them for the first time. Convinced he was being tested, Keepnews soon learned that some jazz players approached record producers as if they were the opposition.

On the third album, "Brilliant Corners," Monk recorded his own music. Considered one of the era's most original jazz albums, it was a nightmare to produce. Using the Reeves Sound Studios in New York for the first time, Keepnews assembled an all-star lineup for Monk, including Rollins, bassist Oscar Pettiford, and drummer Max Roach. But Monk's challenging arrangements continually evolved in the studio, frustrating some of the musicians. The group tried the wildly unorthodox title track (with every other chorus played in double time) more than 25 times and never reached the final bar. Pettiford and Monk argued. At one point, Keepnews thought that the bass microphone malfunctioned, only to realize Pettiford had pantomimed his part. For the album's second session, the band lineup changed, with trumpeter Clark Terry added. Using every minute of

113

his limited studio time, Keepnews scrambled to record enough material for an album, saved by Monk's clever, impromptu piano solo on the standard, "I Surrender Dear."

Conditioned by the many Monk compositions common to jazz, today's listeners may have a difficult time fully appreciating the radical nature of "Brilliant Corners," the first significant jazz album on Riverside. It was a grand rebuttal to music reviewers who had criticized Keepnews for his conservative approach on Monk's first two Riverside releases and a testament to the producer's studio diplomacy and editing skills. Some 40 years later, in the bebop-laden 1990s, "Brilliant Corners" sounds as fresh as ever.

After issuing a solo piano album in early 1957 called "Thelonius Himself," Keepnews later that year produced the only studio recordings of Monk with John Coltrane. For the sessions, leading to the album "Monk's Music," the pianist requested saxophonists Coleman Hawkins, a star from the 1930s, and a 21-year-old Coltrane, who had been working for trumpeter Miles Davis. After Davis allegedly slapped Coltrane in the face, Monk offered Coltrane a job. During the same year, Coltrane fronted a history-making Monk quartet at New York's Five Spot Club.

The album featured Coltrane on Monk's gorgeous ballad "Ruby My Dear," "Crepuscule with Nellie," and "Well, You Needn't," a recording famous for Monk hollering "Coltrane! Coltrane!" to notify the saxophonist to solo. (For years, jazz writers have claimed that Coltrane fell asleep due to the aftereffects of narcotics.) The album's cover design, with a portrait of the ever-cool Monk squeezed into a child's toy wagon, promoted the more established Hawkins, Blakey, and Gigi Grice, not the still-unknown Coltrane. (Reissues from the sessions, however, were billed "Monk/Trane.") Keepnews regrets that other Coltrane and Monk sessions could not be organized. "Coltrane was under contract with Prestige," Keepnews said. "We had a deal where Coltrane could record again [on Riverside], if Monk would appear with Coltrane on Prestige. Monk had a bad experience with Prestige and would have nothing to do with them. So that killed future [Riverside] sessions together."

Up through 1960, Keepnews showcased Monk with superb

lead saxophonists, such as Griffin (on the live albums "Thelonius in Action" and "Misterioso"), Gerry Mulligan, and Charlie Rouse, who played with Monk well into the 1960s. Sales increased steadily with each release. After a successful live session in San Francisco, Monk left Riverside and joined the larger Columbia label. Keepnews and Grauer acquired master tapes of live concerts with Monk in Europe and issued them on Riverside. Ironically, Monk's European draw was bolstered by the many Riverside albums, which helped to further expose him to an overseas audience.

Despite Monk's departure, Riverside by then had found its growing niche with modern jazz listeners with albums by Bill Evans, the Adderly brothers, guitarist Charlie Byrd, Montgomery, Rollins, and many others. Dwarfed by the major labels, Riverside competed at a level with other leading independent jazz labels, such as Prestige, Pacific Jazz, and Blue Note. Riverside survived by producing excellent records while maintaining a low overhead. "We knew we were selling in a limited economy," Keepnews says. "Our cost structure actually made it hard to lose money." For example, he signed musicians with the standard AFM (American Federation of Musicians) union contract form, thus avoiding the need for a lawyer.

"Musicians got the standard 5 percent royalty on sales," Keepnews says. "An album could be memorable or ordinary, but the sales were usually about the same—a few thousand copies. The word [among jazz musicians] in the 1950s was that Blue Note paid musicians for a day rehearsal and a one-day recording session. Prestige paid you to record in one day with no rehearsal, and at Riverside, you were paid for two days of recording and no rehearsal."

Riverside produced polished albums by organizing sessions around players who knew each other. "There was an interconnection between art and commerce because with limited studio time, it was essential to create a rhythm section where everyone was comfortable," Keepnews said. "In other words, you didn't break in new people in the studio." For example, the rhythm section of pianist Wynton Kelly, bassist Sam Jones, and drummer Philly Joe Jones was a staple at Riverside. "Wynton was the best jazz accompanist in the world and a very important contributor," according to Keepnews.

Riverside's cost structure allowed the label to build the musicians' following over several albums. One poor-selling debut album didn't deter Keepnews if a musician was promising. Such was the case with Bill Evans, an introverted white pianist from New Jersey whose model scales and dissonant chord structures shaped jazz harmony in the late 1950s and early 1960s. "Introspective" is a common description for Evans' piano style. His Riverside releases from 1957 through 1963 influenced scores of musicians, including pianists Keith Jarrett, Herbie Hancock, Chick Corea, vibraphonist Gary Burton, and contemporary jazz guitarist Pat Metheny, who once described his approach to music as "a continuation of the Bill Evans school of thought." [4]

A few months after signing Monk to Riverside, Grauer and Keepnews were contacted by guitarist Mundell Lowe. He insisted that they listen, over the telephone, to a demo tape by Evans, who was working in obscurity in Greenwich Village clubs. But Evans was extremely reluctant to record. Keepnews lured him into the studio in 1957, producing his first album, "New Jazz Conception." Total sales after one year: 800 copies. Keepnews pushed for more, but Evans claimed he had nothing new to say. In 1958, Evans joined Miles Davis and played a key role in the trumpeter's landmark Columbia recording "Kind of Blue."

After several months with Davis, Evans left in 1959 and began recording a series of trio sessions for Riverside. "Playing with Miles Davis gave him exposure, which helped to attract attention to his Riverside recordings," Keepnews said. Evans joined bassist Scott LaFaro and drummer Paul Motian to form a trio now regarded as one of jazz's greatest based on their brilliant interplay. Over a two-year period, Keepnews produced four albums by the trio: "Portraits in Jazz," "Explorations," and the live albums "Sunday at the Village Vanguard" and "Waltz for Debby," both recorded on June 25, 1961, during three sets in the club. The live albums are vibrant and spontaneous, with Evans' distinct musical signature on old standards and originals. For Keepnews, the live session was a "relatively painless way to extract an album from the usually foot-dragging pianist." [5] The decision was an important one. LaFaro died in a car accident 10

Little Labels—Big Sound

days after the Village Vanguard engagement, leaving Evans devastated.

Almost a year later, Evans settled on bassist Chuck Israels and actually pursued sessions for Riverside. The change of heart was a mixed blessing for Keepnews. A narcotics addiction prompted Evans to seek cash advances for each session, and Riverside was not flush in cash. "It was difficult to be his friend and co-owner of Riverside during that period," Keepnews said. Despite the circumstances, the Evans trio performed brilliantly on several albums.

In 1962, Keepnews devised the idea of recording two albums at once by having the Evans trio alternate between soft ballads and upbeat tunes. The ballads were packaged for the album "Moonbeams," the show tunes for "How My Heart Sings." Later that year, Evans recorded the "Interplay" album with guitarist Jim Hall and trumpeter Freddie Hubbard, who didn't know many of the standards Evans had selected. Playing with no preconceptions, Hubbard's fresh interpretations suited Evans' approach. Evans joined Verve Records in late 1963, but not before Keepnews produced several sessions of the pianist. Much of the recorded material was not released on Riverside but resurfaced years later on other Keepnews projects. Despite Evans' personal difficulties, Keepnews was his good friend and faithful supporter.

Evans was with Riverside during a great period for the label, both commercially and artistically. Keepnews had signed Cannonball Adderly and Wes Montgomery, both of whom cared about the label's well-being. No one finances jazz records to make a fortune; the endeavor blends business and idealism. Cannonball Adderly's support for Riverside was particularly meaningful to Keepnews.

Clark Terry introduced Keepnews to alto saxophonist Julian "Cannonball" Adderly and his younger brother, trumpeter Nat, at a New York club in 1957. Cannonball, a former high school teacher from Florida, pursued music full-time in the early 1950s after a military stint. In 1955, he and his brother moved to New York and became an integral part of the jazz scene. However, Cannonball was struggling to lead his own commercially viable band. In 1958, he joined Riverside with the stipulation that if he ever organized his own

117

band and felt it was ready to record, Riverside would promptly do so. Initially, Cannonball recorded with Riverside regulars, including Kelly and Blakey. Cannonball also toured and recorded with Miles Davis on the Columbia label, appearing on the "Kind of Blue" and "Milestones" albums.

In 1959, Cannonball organized a quintet with his brother, bassist Sam Jones, drummer Lou Hayes, and pianist Bobby Timmons. After a few weeks together, they headed for the Jazz Workshop in San Francisco, California, and soon announced it was time to record. Through business contacts, Keepnews found an area field producer and headed West. The result, "Cannonball Adderly in San Francisco," was an electrifying live album with a funk feel that sold a staggering 50,000 copies. "We had a real hit, which was a huge lift," Keepnews said. (The Timmons composition "This Here" appeared in jukeboxes.) In all, Keepnews recorded five live albums for Cannonball, who became Riverside's biggest draw.

"When recording live, you lose the element of control, but Cannonball thrived under those circumstances, because he was bigger than life," said Keepnews, who included liberal portions of the saxophonist's dialogue with the audience on the live records. Just at a time when the growing presence of rock music was threatening the market for straight-ahead jazz records, Cannonball's soulful, danceable sound had a broad appeal. Keepnews expected to lose Cannonball to a larger label in 1961 when his Riverside contract expired. But he enjoyed working with Keepnews and also supported the label as a sideman for other Riverside artists. "Cannonball's loyalty to me was unbelievable," Keepnews said. "He was a very special man."

Viewing Riverside as a team enterprise, Cannonball urged Keepnews to sign Wes Montgomery, a father of six children who had been a regular for years in Indianapolis clubs while working day jobs. With his sheer talent, originality, and naturally friendly nature, the Indiana man was immediately accepted by New York's best players. Between 1959 and 1963, Keepnews produced several small group albums of Montgomery, including "The Incredible Jazz Guitar of Wes Montgomery." Like Evans, Montgomery was notoriously self-critical but "never said a bad word about anyone else around him,"

Saxophonist and band leader Julian "Cannonball" Adderly from a Riverside publicity photo. Adderly's funk-styled records were among Riverside's best sellers in the early 1960s.

Keepnews said. Montgomery fronted studio bands with Milt Jackson, George Shearing, Ron Carter, and many others, and also played for Nat Adderly and other Riverside acts. "Wes was never a big seller," Keepnews said, "but the [Riverside] recordings advanced his career.

Today, people prefer his Riverside recordings over his other work. I'm biased, but I agree."

By late 1963, Riverside seemed to be rolling, with dozens of titles available, improved distribution outlets, and Cannonball bordering on pop stardom. In the beginning, Keepnews rarely left Manhattan to record. With the label now more established, Keepnews' circle of jazz associates spanned the country as he managed sessions on both coasts. Then disaster struck in December, just two weeks after the assassination of John F. Kennedy. Bill Grauer, Riverside co-owner and business manager, died unexpectedly of a heart attack at age 42. "He was under a lot of stress," Keepnews said. "In those days, people didn't pay attention to the [health] warning signs."

To Keepnews' dismay, he found Riverside in a web of financial entanglements. "Bill Grauer was a very high-powered guy, an expansionist who had wanted to make Riverside big," Keepnews said. "His death revealed a series of financial maneuvers, but he was no longer there to perform them. I tried my best to work through it, but I had left the financial end of Riverside to Grauer."

By early 1964, Riverside was sinking. Cannonball offered to extend his contract, hoping to provide reassurance to anxious Riverside creditors. "The main trouble was that Riverside was mortgaged up to slightly above eye-level. We were at the mercy of financial types whose shifting attitudes made it quite likely that the label was simply beyond being saved even by Cannon's ploy," Keepnews said. [6]

After considering his friend's offer, Keepnews finally pleaded with Cannonball to move on and advance his career with a larger label. Shortly thereafter, Riverside slid into bankruptcy. To make matters worse, Riverside's extensive master tapes, which represented much of Keepnews' professional achievement since 1955, were used as collateral against company loans and were sold during the proceedings. "We pursued our dream of a jazz label and ended up $3 million in the hole," Keepnews said.

Following his Riverside years, Keepnews enjoyed a long, successful career as a jazz producer, record executive, and writer. Keepnews first became an independent producer for a couple of years. In 1966, despite the continued dominance of rock recording, Keepnews again gambled on modern jazz, creating the Milestone label, with Dick Katz as a partner. The New York–based company produced albums by such notable saxophonists as Lee Konitz and Joe Henderson. In 1972, Keepnews attracted pianist McCoy Tyner to the label, resulting in more than a dozen albums over the decade.

By 1973, music acquisitions by the long-running Fantasy Records label enabled Keepnews to launch an explosion in jazz reissue anthologies. The Berkeley, California–based company, which profited in the early 1970s with the big-ticket rock act Credence Clearwater Revival, moved aggressively into jazz by purchasing Prestige, Riverside, and Milestone. Keepnews directed jazz productions for Fantasy and moved permanently to San Francisco, a city that had first captivated him when he did live Riverside sessions in the early 1960s.

While overseeing new albums for Milestone (adding Sonny Rollins and Ron Carter to the label in the mid-1970s), Keepnews compiled more than 200 double-album jazz reissue compilations (called "twofers") under the Fantasy, Milestone, and Prestige banners. He dipped into his Riverside material, including numerous unreleased outtakes and finished performances. In the 1970s, the last decade dominated by vinyl albums, the specially priced anthologies put vital jazz back into circulation for a new generation of listeners. Some "twofers," such as Bill Evans' original Riverside material, sold better the second time around. Other jazz labels soon emulated the Fantasy concept. "There is more than a little love involved in all of this," wrote Fantasy executive Ralph Gleason in 1975. "To watch Orrin come roaring out of the vault, clutching a reel of tape he had forgotten sounded as good as it does because he hadn't heard it in 20 years, is a delightful experience." [7]

In 1980, Keepnews resigned as vice president at Fantasy to devote more time to producing albums. In 1985, he created the Landmark Records label. In recent years, Keepnews has gone full circle, focusing on jazz writing. With the creation of boxed CD sets, Keepnews produced and wrote extensive liner notes for the complete Riverside recordings by Evans, Montgomery, and Monk. Keepnews' liner notes for the Evans boxed set won him a Grammy Award in 1983. Five years later, Oxford University Press published the ac-

121

After turning his love for jazz music into a profession, Orrin Keepnews co-founded the Riverside label in New York and produced several landmark recordings in the 1950s and early 1960s.

claimed, *The View from Within*, a collection of Keepnews' jazz writings from 1948 through 1987, beginning with his earliest pieces in *The Record Changer*.

There's a clear sense of poetic justice in Keepnews' career in record producing. While promoting music for a niche audience, he produced scores of modest-selling jazz albums greatly overshadowed by the pop hits of the day. Unlike the long-forgotten hit parade of years past, his Riverside albums are very much with us today, both in terms of musical relevance and availability on CD. In the 1940s, Keepnews first noticed the remarkable shelf life of jazz records when collectors began coveting the rare, hot jazz 78-rpm discs of the 1920s. The same staying power has held true with his work. "Popular music tends to have a short life," Keepnews says. "What sells well in its day may later have you wondering what the fuss was all about. Jazz has a long life, perhaps, because of its spontaneity. It's incredibly rewarding to see the records still around (in print) after many, many years."

Eight / **Ace Records**

"Man, they won't pay you; we will. It's impossible to pay anybody three cents a record."

—John Vincent of Ace Records to Guitar Slim

Forty years ago, John Vincent sold plastic dreams from an office in Jackson, Mississippi, and became one of the original rock 'n' roll hit makers. His label, Ace Records, embodied the burgeoning 1950s record business, which was fast, hot, lean, and driven by 45-rpm singles, disc jockeys, and jukeboxes. Vincent was important to the development of New Orleans rhythm and blues (R&B) and his Ace label was also among the first labels to bring the music to the young rock 'n' roll audience, recording such artists as pianists Huey Smith, Eddie Bo, Dr. John, and James Booker, guitarist Earl King, and teenage pop idol Frankie Ford, whose hit rendition of Smith's "Sea Cruise" became an anthem for the Crescent City.

Vincent knew that New Orleans R&B would have a national appeal. While headquartered 150 miles away in Jackson, Ace was essentially a New Orleans label that promoted local and regional musicians. Today, it seems old-fashioned: a company that depended on local talent to survive. But Vincent valued the New Orleans sound so much that he gambled his own career and money to form Ace, which became New Orleans' first national record label and a model for Minit and other New Orleans record companies in the late 1950s and early 1960s.

Like other small labels catering to R&B and rock 'n' roll in the 1950s, Ace possessed a company cockiness that reflected its flamboyant owner. It was an era when a small regional label could mirror the personality of its creator and still make an impact on a national scale. If Vincent had not found the record business, he might have found used cars or the psychic hot lines. He could sell and make people believe in themselves. Dr. John, a producer and arranger at Ace in the 1950s, once described Vincent as a con artist and record hustler. Even today, when Vincent's Mississippi tongue drawls with a well-worn music story, his eyes flash and, for a moment, even the most squeaky-voiced observer believes he is capable of recording a jukebox hit.

Producing some 200 singles on Ace in the 1950s and early 1960s, Vincent recorded everything from blues to pop to rockabilly, depending upon his whim and the latest radio fad. In 1955, Vincent asked Sam Phillips, owner of Sun Records in Memphis, about a

125

young Elvis Presley, whose records on Sun had not yet broken nationally. "I asked, 'Does Elvis sell?' " said Vincent, recalling his conversation with Phillips. "He [Phillips] said, 'Johnny, it's a most mysterious thing. He has sold about 35,000 copies.' I said, 'Man, that's what I'm going into!' Then I heard about doo-wop selling, and I tried that, too. I've been a versatile guy. But no matter if we recorded a commercial New York sound or an LA sound or whatever, we always put a New Orleans feel to it." [1]

John Vincent Imbragulio's passion for music began soon after his birth on October 3, 1925, in rural Laurel, Mississippi. As a boy, the son of Phillip and Tina Imbragulio helped in their small restaurant, but more often he was in front of their glowing jukebox. "In high school, I didn't date many girls," he said in 1995, "I just played records. That's all I lived for. Something fascinated me about records. I was never a musician, but I learned to play the radio. I had only enough money to buy two or three records on a Saturday, but those were all blues—by Big Boy Crudup and guys like him, who I learned were all livin' here in Mississippi. That made me even more interested."

In 1946, after Vincent returned to Laurel from military service, he opened a jukebox business and, later, a record store, selling mostly black records for local bar operators. He was not well educated, and the music business seemed preferable to manual labor. Though he barely made enough money to support his growing family, Vincent was hooked on records and how they were made. He played the same 78-rpm discs for hours to analyze the singers' phrasing and the instrumentation.

Vincent's interest peaked just as the tiny J&M Recording Service began operating about 150 miles away in New Orleans. J&M soon had a major impact on Vincent. The studio was founded by Cosimo Matassa, who had operated an appliance store in the French Quarter. For additional income, Matassa sold used records from his father's jukeboxes. As more customers asked for new titles, Matassa dropped appliances and opened the J&M Music Shop. He added a Duo Press disc cutter and other primitive recording equipment in a back room, and his J&M Recording Service soon began catering to

Little Labels—Big Sound

school bands, glee clubs, and choirs. Gradually, nightclub singers found the studio. In 1947, David Braun of New Jersey's DeLuxe Records brought in Paul Gayten to record his hit, "True." Later that year, DeLuxe recorded Annie Laurie's ballad "Since I Fell for You." Black artists walked into J&M to record the New Orleans R&B sound —a blend of jazz-oriented rhythms, soulful blues, and hot, humid weather.

Following J&M's activities from a distance, Vincent wanted to enter the record-making end of the business in any capacity. He read that a New Orleans record distributor, William B. Allen Music Sales, needed a representative to cover sales for rural Alabama, Louisiana, and Mississippi. To Vincent's surprise, the company hired him. While he sold other peoples' records, he began producing his own releases. Traveling on the job for Allen Music Sales, Vincent would pull into tiny Southern towns, round up obscure blues and hillbilly singers and take them back to Jackson to record in Lillian McMurray's little Trumpet Records studio. Vincent's productions, pressed on his own small Champion label (with the slogan: "It's a Knockout Champion Record"), sold only a few hundred copies, but the experience taught Vincent the inner workings of a recording studio and how to handle musicians.

"I went over to see Big Boy Crudup, and I got the nerve to ask him to record for me," Vincent said. "He said, 'Just give me $25.' Now, that was *my* kind of money. I took him over to WRBC Radio in Jackson and we cut six sides. There were few recording studios around here then." Since Crudup (whose "That's All Right, Mama" was later recorded by Elvis Presley) already recorded for other companies, Vincent listed him as "Arthur Blues Crump and His Guitar."

These were wild days in the record business. Vincent sensed that R&B music was evolving and attitudes in the segregated South were changing. "In Mississippi back then, a lot of people didn't want me to put R&B records on their jukeboxes," Vincent said. "But the [white] kids enjoyed the music. The work used to be dangerous. Once, I went over to get a black guy to record, and his boss was there. He came out with a big shotgun and asked me, 'What you doin' here? You come here to get my nigger?' I said, 'No, sir. He was supposed to record for me, but I was waitin' for him to get off work first.' The guy said, 'Now, listen, I advise you to get in your car and don't let it stop.' I said, 'Sir, you don't have to worry about *my* car stoppin.' I won't be comin' back over here again.' "

By 1949, Vincent learned all he could from William B. Allen, so he opened his own distribution company at 241 North Farish St., in a black neighborhood in Jackson. The small operation provided a living, but he was still limited to record distribution. He longed to record the many blues artists in the city and rural clubs. Meanwhile, nearby New Orleans jumped with its own sounds: jazz, zydeco, blues, and the evolving R&B sound. Nightclubs popped up on every corner and stayed open around the clock, creating shift work for musicians.

The small independent labels were the first to promote the New Orleans R&B sound. In 1949, Lewis Chudd's Imperial Records in Los Angeles hired New Orleans trumpeter Dave Bartholomew to produce local musicians. That first year, Bartholomew wrote Jewel King's hit release, "3 x 7 = 21," for the label. Chudd signed several Crescent City performers for Imperial, including Big Joe Turner, Roy Brown (composer of "Good Rockin' Tonight"), Smiley Lewis, Tommy Ridgley, and the Spiders. But most notably, Bartholomew eventually co-wrote and arranged many of Fats Domino's smash hits on Imperial.

In Los Angeles, Art Rupe at Specialty Records shook his head in frustration. His main competitor, Imperial, had scored a major coup in New Orleans. Worse, the aggressive Syd Nathan at King Records also pursued the Crescent City sound. Rupe decided to open a New Orleans office and hire a local record chief. Advertising in trade publications, he received inquiries from experienced record men, but a New Orleans distributor recommended Vincent. In 1952, Rupe traveled to Jackson and offered Vincent the job. A natural candidate, Vincent knew the back roads and the regional music scene. However, Rupe thought Imbragulio was too long a name for the record business. He preferred a more flashy name with fewer syllables—Johnny Vincent.

"He said he'd pay me $587 a month," said Vincent, whose role

128

Little Labels—Big Sound

with Specialty soon expanded beyond the New Orleans area. "He [Rupe] said, 'If you go out for entertainment, *always* go in the daytime. It's cheaper.' So I did. I jumped right into it, and pretty soon, Rupe asked me to cut John Lee Hooker in Detroit, the Soul Stirrers in Little Rock, Lloyd Price in Washington, D.C., and bluesman Frankie Lee Sims in Dallas. I went all over the country promoting and producing records for Specialty. I guess I got a lot of sins on me because of old Rupe. He made me sign many artists for a half-cent royalty a record. If an artist sold a million copies, he wouldn't have $3,000 coming after taxes and expenses. It was pitiful."

In his own backyard, Vincent signed to Specialty the popular Eddie "Guitar Slim" Jones, dubbed the "New Orleans blues sensation." Never mind that Atlantic Records offered Jones three cents a record. Waving a big cigar, Vincent told Slim, "Man, they won't pay you; we will. It's impossible to pay anybody three cents a record." Vincent liked Slim's flashy, cocky style. Slim, who wore red suits and dyed his hair to match, combined gospel and blues with a screeching guitar that was a precursor for modern rock guitar. Vincent took Slim to Matassa's studio and produced four sides, including Slim's original "The Things That I Used to Do," a moody blues number that topped the R&B charts in 1952 and later became part of the standard blues repertoire. Although Slim failed to produce other hits for Specialty, "The Things That I Used to Do" established Vincent as a hot producer and wheeler-dealer.

But Vincent wasn't satisfied. Rupe would become upset if Imperial or other labels scooped Specialty with a new act who hit the charts. By early 1955, Vincent was tired of working for someone else and wanted his own operation again. Then, there was an issue over money. As a Specialty record producer (the term had not come into popular use yet), Vincent claimed he was owed a penny for every record sold. He estimated that the amount owed him was so large that Rupe had little choice but to fire him in an "austerity" move. A sympathetic Rupe asked an Atlanta distributor to hire Vincent.

"Rupe gave me a jolt, firin' me," Vincent said. "I came back to Mississippi and wondered what I was gonna do. I went up to Memphis to see a friend, Les Birhari, who owned a little label called

129

Meteor. Les said, 'So what's next?' I said, 'I'm gonna start me a label.' He said, 'What you gonna call it?' Well, my hair was messed up at the time, and I pulled out my comb and happened to look at it. It was an Ace comb. So I told Les, 'I'm going to call my label Ace.' I went back to New Orleans and got to work. I knew where to find the artists. I figured I'd cut some blues stuff. I bumped into Huey 'Piano' Smith, and he wanted to go with me. So did Earl King. I took them from Specialty."

Vincent set up a distribution network and ordered a company logo on sheer nerve. His first release, "Shuckin'" and "I Got the Blues for You" (Ace 500) by Al Collins, is rarely heard today, although it occasionally appears on reissue R&B anthologies. Collins' record received regional attention, but the straightforward blues number could never be a national hit in early 1955, not with its suggestive reference to a woman's anatomy. Vincent followed up with R&B records by New Orleans guitarist Earl King and singer Eddie Bo. A pioneer of 1950s New Orleans R&B, King was the son of a local blues player. He first sang in church, but graduated to smoky nightclubs by age 15. He learned to play guitar by watching Guitar Slim and soon attracted an audience around town. His first record, an original blues song called "Mother's Love," became a regional hit for Specialty in 1954. The next year, Vincent invited King to Jackson to record his "Those Lonely, Lonely Nights," a two-chord ballad with a pleasing blues feel and a catchy melody. It became Ace Records' first national success, reaching seventh on *Billboard*'s R&B chart. The record caught the ear of R&B performer Johnny "Guitar" Watson, who covered the same song on the more prominent Modern label, limiting Ace's sales of King's rendition to 250,000 copies. But the song helped Ace build a reputation for R&B and encouraged King to write and record new material for Ace and Vincent's subsidiary Vin label.

King's "Everybody Has to Cry Sometime" on Vin sold about 70,000 copies in the region, with King dubbed as Handsome Earl. For a brief time, King was a national attraction. His subsequent Ace records, however, generated little interest outside the Gulf Coast area. In the early 1960s, King scored some minor hits on Imperial.

Little Labels—Big Sound

Today, he continues the New Orleans R&B tradition by performing and serving as the city's unofficial music historian, a link to the city's colorful past. His songs have been recorded by Jimi Hendrix, Dr. John, Stevie Ray Vaughn, Lee Dorsey, and numerous other artists.

With the $10,000 profit netted from King's "Those Lonely, Lonely Nights," Vincent expanded his roster of musicians and began recording them in Matassa's New Orleans studio. A profitable friendship ensued and they became partners in small projects, while Matassa continued to rent the studio to other labels. With Matassa handling the engineering, the studio turned out national hits for Fats Domino on Imperial. Matassa's session players included some of New Orleans' best: Huey Smith, piano; Earl Palmer, drums; Earl Smith, guitar; Earl Fields, bass; Ernest McLean, guitar; Lee Allen, tenor saxophone; and Red Tyler, baritone saxophone and leader of the studio band.

Matassa's studio was integral to the success of Ace and the New Orleans sound. It produced a clear, deep, and funky sound that Matassa attributed to the weather. "Down here, it's so humid that if you stand in one place too long, you'll turn green and take root," he said. [2] In 1956, he moved to a larger building at 523 Governor Nicholls St.

That year, Mac Rebennack, an original pianist who now performs as Dr. John, joined Ace as a producer and recording artist. He viewed Vincent as a country bumpkin, perhaps because Vincent would fire Rebennack, then rehire him a few weeks later. "Johnny Vincent was a very good con artist," he wrote. "For instance, if the session was with Huey Smith, he'd say, 'Huu-ree, put some *shit* into it.' And everybody would respond and, sure enough, put some shit into it. That was it; that was the compiled wisdom of Johnny Vincent's approach to making records." [3]

But the approach somehow worked. By the time Rebennack left Ace permanently in 1957, the label had reached the national charts with Huey Smith's "Rockin' Pneumonia and the Boogie Woogie Flu." Although it reached only 52nd on the *Billboard* pop chart, it became a jukebox favorite and a top R&B release that summer.

The following year, Smith finally broke into both the pop and R&B top 10 with "Don't You Just Know It" and "High Blood Pressure." Ace was rolling and Vincent obtained valuable copyrights for his Ace Publishing (BMI) music catalog. With Specialty, Imperial, Ace, and other small labels producing the New Orleans sound, the nation's music establishment paid attention.

When "Don't You Just Know It" broke nationally, Vincent took a telephone call from Sam Clark, head of ABC Records. Vincent recalled: "I caught the train to Philly to hear him out. Mr. Clark said, 'We'll give you $50,000 [for rights to the recording]. Think about it. Look, if you don't sell us the record, we're gonna cut the song with Lloyd Price. You gonna lose the record.' I went to the telephone and called Buster Williams, who had a pressing plant in Memphis, and I said, 'Buster, they offered me $50,000. What do you think I ought to do?' He said, 'Do you want to be in the record business, son?' I said, 'Yes, sir!' He said, 'Then I'll press all you want and give you unlimited credit. All you have to do is give me all your business.' I said, 'Buster, you got it *all*.' "

A worried Vincent then visited Dick Clark, the biggest force in rock 'n' roll and host of ABC Television's *American Bandstand*. Dick Clark apparently heard about ABC Records' threat to cover "Don't You Just Know It" and assured Vincent that he would not allow it. Clark ultimately became an Ace supporter and promoted its artists on his show.

In Huey Smith, Ace had a distinctive performer who learned his trade from the top New Orleans R&B players of the 1940s and early 1950s. Born in 1934 in New Orleans' Garden District, Smith was influenced by Professor Longhair, the city's offbeat piano inno-vator. Smith also discovered blues records by Bull Moose Jackson, Ivory Joe Hunter, and Louis Jordan. At 15, he joined Guitar Slim's blues band and played regional clubs. When Slim found new band members in 1954, Smith started his own group and did session work at J&M. Like his contemporary, pianist-singer Fats Domino, Smith had a recognizable piano style. While Domino was known for his bright, rhythmic boogie, Smith perfected a shuffling right-handed break on the piano often imitated by Southern players. His piano

132

style was well suited for session work, and he played on many releases from New Orleans in the late 1950s and early 1960s.

Working with his own band, the Clowns, Smith left most of the singing to Junior Gordon, Roland Stone, and Bobby Marchan. Smith concentrated on writing commercial songs, using clichés, street talk, and rhymes to produce oddly named songs such as "Don't You Know, Yockomo" and "Chicken Wah Wah." The band packed the regional black clubs, and, for a few years, enjoyed a national following. During the band's heyday in the late 1950s, a main draw was Marchan, a Youngstown, Ohio, native who arrived in New Orleans in the early 1950s with a group of female impersonators called The Powder Box Revue. (After leaving the Clowns, he carved a good career out of personal appearances, and in the 1970s, he wrote "Body English" for King Floyd and "Get Down Get with It" for Slade.)

Because of his late 1950s recordings on Ace, Smith is now regarded as one of the great band leaders in early rock. Sadly, he soon faded from the music scene. He battled Vincent for royalty payments in the 1960s after he had left Ace for Imperial. While Smith was with Imperial, Vincent released one of Smith's earlier Ace tracks, "The Popeye," based on a popular dance. The record sold well regionally, and eventually Smith returned to Ace. But Smith and Vincent failed to recapture the old fire. After playing in New Orleans clubs in the 1960s, Smith left the business. For years he worked as a janitor and gardener. He became a Jehovah's Witness. A comeback in the late 1970s failed. In the 1990s, he has been a reclusive figure living in a small house in Baton Rouge. Vincent said Smith sold the rights to many of his songs for practically nothing.

During Smith's peak years at Ace, Vincent also turned to the growing white teenage market. Like other record label owners, Vincent was fascinated by the success of Elvis Presley and the Sun rockabilly movement. In 1958, Vincent "discovered" handsome 17-year-old Jimmy Clanton while he recorded demos with his band, the Rockets, in Matassa's studio. Matassa, who managed the singer's career, teamed with Vincent in the studio to produce Clanton's "Just a Dream," which reached both the R&B and pop charts that July. Two films and other big hits on the Ace label followed, including "A

Part of Me," "Go, Jimmy, Go," and "Venus in Blue Jeans." With Clanton, Vincent's little Mississippi label finally had a white teen idol and one of the South's big-name singers in early rock.

In 1959, Vincent found another 17-year-old, Frank Guzzo, of suburban Gretna, Louisiana, an aspiring white soul singer who loved Frank Sinatra. Vincent gave him the stage name Frankie Ford, apparently because Ford cars were popular. The singer's manager, Joe Caronna, set up a session at Matassa's studio to record "Cheatin' Woman" and "Last One to Cry." The record sold well in New Orleans and received sporadic airplay on black stations in Philadelphia, leading to live bookings there. Ford remembered arriving in Philadelphia for The Georgie Woods Show at the Uptown Theater. "Georgie saw me and said, 'Hey, man, you're a white guy!' I said, 'Well, nobody's perfect.' But he let me sing, and the black audience really liked me. I knew I could entertain anybody." [4]

Ford's big break came with the Ace release "Sea Cruise," which attracted white and black listeners. Huey Smith, the song's composer, first recorded "Sea Cruise" on Matassa's two-track recorder, with Marchan on lead vocals. Smith wanted to issue the record for his band, the Clowns, but Vincent had other plans. Since Marchan planned to leave the band, Vincent added Ford's vocals to the track and released "Sea Cruise" under his name. Vincent thought the record's flip side, "Roberta," was the show stopper, and it initially received the most air play. "Those were the greatest tracks I ever produced," Vincent said. "By now things were going great for Ace. It seemed we could do nothing wrong."

When ABC's Dick Clark began promoting "Sea Cruise," the song climbed the charts. The record was instantly recognizable by its good-time Mardi Gras rhythm, fog horn, ship's bell introduction, and infectious chorus of "ooo-wee, ooo-wee, baby." One can almost imagine passing through New Orleans to the Gulf of Mexico. A favorite on rock oldies stations, "Sea Cruise" remains so familiar today that most people assume it was a number one record. Actually, it peaked at 14th on the *Billboard* pop chart and seventh on the R&B chart in April 1959. As the record obtained national air play, many listeners assumed Ford was black. "He wanted me to sound black,"

Johnny Vincent, owner of Ace Records, merged the voice of a white teenager, Frankie Ford, with the music of New Orleans R&B band leader Huey Smith to create the national hit "Sea Cruise" in 1959.

Ford said of Vincent. "In fact, after the record started hitting and I went to Philadelphia to promote it, people were expecting to see a black guy. Of course, coming from New Orleans, I was no stranger to working with black musicians. The record laid around for seven months before Dick Clark picked it up and it took off. When I think of how one song impacted my life, it's incredible. It launched a lifelong career. *Rolling Stone* said the record was the greatest marriage of music and material. It just cooked. Other people have recorded it over the years, including Johnny Rivers, but his was just an LA copy. Mine had that old New Orleans sound." [5]

During the label's halcyon days of the late 1950s and early 1960s, Ace remained essentially a singles label. Huey Smith, Clanton, and Ford provided Ace with considerable national recognition, but Vincent also recorded numerous R&B singles by regional musicians. Among the more notable was James Booker, the talented "Piano Prince" and regular studio sideman who influenced such diverse keyboard players as Dr. John and George Winston. Known as the "king of the left-handed rhythm," Booker backed singer Joe Tex during Tex's brief tenure at Ace. (Tex's career expanded in Nashville in the mid-1960s.) Other interesting Ace artists included Alvin "Red" Tyler, Jimmy "Mercy Baby" Mullins (drummer for Frankie Lee Sims), Joe and Ann, and Bobby Fields. New Orleans' R&B well ran so deep that Vincent could pick from any number of eager performers, including the blues harp man Sammy Myers, who cut "Sleeping in the Ground" with the King Mose Royal Rockers. Although Ace produced few albums, some are now collectible, including "Just a Dream," by Jimmy Clanton, "Having a Good Time" by Huey "Piano" Smith & His Clowns, and, of course, "Let's Take a Sea Cruise" by Frankie Ford.

By the early 1960s, New Orleans R&B faced intense competition from the youth-oriented music emerging from other regions. Major labels rushed into the youth record market. Like other independent labels, such as Sun, Duke, and King, Ace battled for air play. As Ace turned increasingly to pop music and depended less on its R&B base, the label's future was doomed. Vincent simply lacked the financial clout to compete in the pop market. The quality of Ace's songs declined, forcing Frankie Ford to record inferior material that failed to exploit his talents.

In 1962, Vincent thought he found the answer to his predicament: a merger with the stronger Vee-Jay Records of Chicago. He signed a five-year contract that called for Vee-Jay to assume control of Ace sales, promotion, and distribution. Vincent planned to produce and develop new acts for both labels. He was to receive a guaranteed $500,000 a year for five years. In a *Billboard* story, Vincent announced: "It's the only real answer for an indie record company today. We simply did not have the power to keep pushing out the volume of releases that give you a chance of having a continuing string of hits. And if you don't have a string of them, the little guy, like me, gets hung up for money. The distributors will eat you alive. That's been our problem . . . the result was that we just had to eat our returns." [6]

Initially, the merger was promising. Improved distribution helped Clanton's "Venus in Blue Jeans," a Neil Sedaka and Howard Greenfield tune, sell more than a million copies. But by 1965, Vincent's happiness had turned to grief. Vee-Jay suffered from the same industry conditions and failed to fulfill its promises to Vincent. When the label was sold to new owners, Vincent did not receive the money he felt he was owed and could not retrieve his Ace master recordings. When the Beatles in 1963–64 launched the British music invasion, American independent labels fell on hard times. Vee-Jay was forced to close. (Ironically, Vee-Jay in early 1963 issued recordings by the Beatles in the United States with limited success. Later that year, the Beatles became a sensation in the United States on the larger Capitol label.)

"We lost it all," Vincent said. "I had intended to go back to New Orleans to run a distributorship, but it laid an egg. I decided to go into the real estate business. Unfortunately, nothing worked for me. I bet I opened 75 to 100 businesses over the years to come—clothing stores, restaurants, health studio, a tile company, you name it. Well, in 1970 a company in Memphis wanted to get into the record business, and its officers wanted me to help them. It got me back in. Finally, I came back here to Jackson, broke. My wife divorced me. I began to do crazy things. I sold the publishing rights to songs for almost nothing. I sold 'Sea Cruise,' 'Just A Dream,' 'Rockin' Pneumonia.' I sold them all for $20,000, which I promptly blew. Oh, man, it was terrible times."

Vincent always felt incomplete without a hand in the record business. Finally, in 1990, a shirt factory owner in Jackson offered financial backing to restart Ace, and Vincent eventually assumed full control of the operation. Now well into his 70s, Vincent operates in a nondescript, brown office park in suburban Pearl, near Jackson. With no outside sign, the cramped office looks like any anonymous corner of the business world. Inside, however, are gold records, publishing awards, and colorful album jackets from the 1950s and 1960s. They bear the recognizable Ace logo with block letters on a musical scale flanked by notes and playing card symbols.

"Now, we're doing $2 million to $3 million a year [in sales]," Vincent said. "This time, it seems everything I've done has been right. I sell some of the old R&B and other stuff and make new records. I still love making records. I have diabetes, cataracts, and heart trouble, but I will keep going. The record company is all I have left, except for my four kids. I can honestly say that the biggest thrill of my life has been the music business. For me, it all comes down to this scene from years ago: I'm walking down the street in New York City and I hear one of my records playing on a radio — a record that I produced. Me, a little old country boy from Laurel, Mississippi, a town of 18,000. Now, that is heaven. You know, people are still askin': How in the dickens did that guy cut all those records?"

Nine / **Monument Records**

"If you're crazy enough, I'm crazy enough."

—Kris Kristofferson's response when Fred Foster proposed he sing for the Monument label

On March 25, 1960, Fred Foster walked into RCA's Studio B in Nashville to produce a struggling singer-songwriter named Roy Orbison. As a rockabilly singer for Sun Records in Memphis in the 1950s, Orbison recorded the moderately successful "Ooby Dooby." But nothing much happened with his career, and now he was recording for Foster's new label, Monument Records.

Even before Harold Bradley and Hank Garland started tuning their guitars, and Buddy Harman had finished tightening his drums, Foster knew something important would happen in the little studio where he had been recording hits for Monument for two years. After the session band and six string players finished their background tracks, Foster turned to Orbison and said, "Here's your first one," meaning his first big hit.

"Are you sure?" Orbison asked.

"I'll pay you a million right now if you'll let me keep the rest," Foster said.

"Are you kidding?"

"No, I'm not."

"Well," Orbison said slowly, "I'd better not do *that*." [1]

Foster laughed when he told the story with total recall. "I was just joking," he said. "But that's how sure I was of that record." Three months after its release, Orbison's "Only the Lonely (Know the Way I Feel)," Monument 421, achieved Foster's expectations: a number two pop record on the *Billboard* charts. It helped launch 19 charted singles for Orbison on Monument through mid-1965, despite the industry upheaval caused by the British rock invasion.

Hits came easily for Orbison and Monument, which Foster started with $1,200 in 1958. Over the next three decades, Monument held its own against the major labels by recording a mix of country, soul, and pop music, primarily by Southern artists. The label produced charted songs up until its sale to Columbia Records in 1986.

The catalyst for Monument's success was Foster, an unorthodox but good-natured label owner who cared about his artists. With his more important performers, Foster was involved in the studio, producing the sessions himself. He wrote many of the album liner notes. He was credited with introducing the first written arrangements to Nashville's studios in the late 1950s. Musicians knew him as a businessman who never compromised his tastes for money. His easygoing style enabled him to make friends in the Nashville music establishment, and he discovered struggling musicians and song-writers and refined their sounds.

Under Foster's guidance, Monument became the thinking man's independent label. Tall and broad-shouldered with a low-key, mannerly style, Foster was a human divining rod, blessed with the ability to point out quirky talent. His company slogan, "Monument Is Artistry," was not corporate hyperbole. As an extension of Foster's musical interests, the label released everything from stone-country Grandpa Jones to soulful Joe Simon. Along the way, Monument's roster included singers Dolly Parton, Willie Nelson, Rusty Draper, Harlan Howard, Billy Walker, Jeanne Seely, Dennis Linde, Larry Gatlin, Kris Kristofferson, Ray Stevens, Henson Cargill, Tony Joe White, Billy Swan, Billy Gammer, steel guitarist Jerry Byrd, trum-peter and arranger Cam Mullins, harmonica player Charlie McCoy, and longtime saxophonist Boots Randolph.

Many Monument releases were steeped in the white and black musical roots of the South. But just when Foster seemed to be recording exclusively in the Southern musical genres, he would surprise everyone with releases by actor Robert Mitchum or 1950s pop singer Don Cherry. While many labels routinely followed hits with soundalike records, Foster's philosophy was to produce good music from unusual singers and songwriters. Ignoring convention, he did what pleased his ears, and that was usually different. And he still made money.

Although he receives little recognition today, Foster produced some of America's more influential pop records, owned two major Nashville studios, and operated a leading song publishing company. He influenced the transformation of Nashville from strictly a coun-try music haven to today's eclectic American music center. From Music Row's boardrooms to its high-tech studios today, Foster's in-fluence is still felt.

Foster was born on July 26, 1931, in Rutherford County, North Carolina, destined not to make music, but to be a farmer as his father was. Country music was nothing more to his family than a respite from the harsh routine of rural life. After his father died, 15-year-old Foster plowed the fields for two years, while dreaming of moving to Washington, D.C., where his sister worked for the federal government. "Our farm was more than 300 acres of row crops," he said. "I knew I didn't want to continue farming."

In the late 1940s, he joined his sister in Washington and found work in a Hot Shoppes restaurant in the Marriott chain. In a short time, he went from car hop to kitchen manager to director of the commissary. "I had a great job," Foster said. "I learned a lot about people and business. They wanted to train me for high-level management, but I told Mr. Marriott I couldn't waste his money. I wanted to learn the music business. For that honor, I ended up taking a pay cut–from $130 a week to $45."

First came a retail sales job at Irving Music, a record store, and then one in promotion with Schwartz Brothers distributors. During his record shop days, he met country singer Jimmy Dean, who was performing at the Covered Wagon, a Washington nightclub. Foster recorded some demos for Dean, which led to Dean's contract with 4 Star Records in Pasadena.

Foster ended up working in East Coast promotion for Mercury Records, where he learned the business from such competitors as Archie Bleyer of Cadence Records and Ahmet Ertegun of Atlantic. In 1956, Mercury executives sent Foster to Nashville to determine why the company sold so few country records. He checked sales records in stores all over the South, and concluded that Mercury's old-fashioned country sound and lack of drums stifled sales. Foster suggested that Mercury update its sound to compete with the stronger beat of rockabilly music, but the label refused. Frustrated by its inaction, he accepted the job of East Coast representative for ABC-Paramount, a new Washington-based label headed by Sam Clark.

"Sam Clark, a wonderful man, said 'Your first order of business is to find us a top–10 record,' " Foster recalled. "So I told Buddy Deane, a top disc jockey in Baltimore and a dear friend, that if he saw anything that could be acquired, he should call me. At 5:30 A.M. on a Saturday he called and said, 'You want a hit, you'd better get over

Little Labels—Big Sound

here.' I didn't even shave. I drove straight to Baltimore. Buddy said, 'Watch this,' and he put a record on. The phones went crazy. I didn't think much of the record, to be honest, but I saw the reaction. So I tracked down the owner in Chapel Hill, North Carolina, flew down there on a Sunday, and on Monday I closed a deal for 'A Rose and a Baby Ruth' by George Hamilton IV. It was our first top–10."

At ABC-Paramount, Foster's ear earned him a reputation. He helped sign Lloyd Price and acquired Ken Copeland's "Pledge of Love." Because he was in the Army, Copeland couldn't pull together his band on the B side of the record. For that reason ABC-Paramount rejected the master, which Imperial Records later obtained and made a hit.

Tired of bureaucracy and constant traveling, Foster left ABC-Paramount to join Baltimore's J & F Wholesale Record Distributors in January 1958. He managed the struggling pop music department. By now, rock 'n' roll had grown from its humble roots to become big-money music, challenging country and adult pop. A big classical label major and J & F client, London Records, wanted to become a pop giant. Foster knew that meant trouble. In March, Walt Maguire, London sales manager, unveiled to J & F employees the label's spring releases. "Suddenly he turned to me and said, 'And you, by the way, are doing a lousy job,' " Foster recalled. "I said, 'Well, you don't give me anything to work with — David Whitfield, Vera Lynn, Frank Chacksfield. The stuff is dated.' "

"He said, 'If you can do better, why don't you?' He was upset. I said, 'I will, then.' So the next day, I started Monument Records and Combine Music. I looked for songs and didn't find anything until August. I found what I thought was an old folk song, which had some archaic language and only two verses. It was called 'Done Laid Around.' I changed the title to 'Gotta Travel On,' wrote a third verse, came down to Nashville, and cut it with Billy Grammer."

Grammer, singer and former lead guitarist for Jimmy Dean's band, recorded the song with a now-famous session group: Chet Atkins, lead guitar; Floyd Cramer, piano; Harold Bradley, rhythm guitar; Bob Moore, bass; Buddy Harman, drums; and the Anita Kerr Quartet on background vocals. Spending all but $80 of his initial

$1,200 investment, Foster returned to Washington, called Maguire, and said, "You asked me to do better, and I did." Maguire proclaimed the song a hit, and offered to release it on Feldsted, a London subsidiary label.

"No, you won't," Foster said. "It goes on Monument."

"What's that?" Maguire said.

"My label."

"I don't think we can do that."

"Well, then you can't have it."

Foster knew he couldn't distribute the record, but his desire to start his own label permitted no compromise. Maguire asked two supervisors for permission to distribute the record on Monument, but they refused. Risking his job, Maguire appealed directly to Sir Edward Lewis, chairman of British Decca and London's founder, who accepted Monument as the first independently owned label to be distributed by London.

Monument's contract with London was for distribution, not financing. When he discovered "Gotta Travel On" was not in the public domain, Foster and his wife had to affix stickers to thousands of individual record labels, crediting folk singer Paul Clayton as the composer, because they couldn't afford to press more records. Disc jockeys did not mind the stickers, however, and in three months the record sold almost a million copies. By the fall of 1958, Monument Records, named for the Washington Monument, had a national hit.

Accustomed to Nashville, Foster returned to RCA's Studio B with Atkins and the band to record Monument's second top–10 hit, "The Shag (Is Totally Cool)." Foster co-wrote the song with Dick Flood for singer Billy Graves to celebrate a dance called The Shag. More hits followed: "Bonaparte's Retreat," by Billy Grammer; "The Three Bells," by Dick Flood; "Theme From 'Adventures in Paradise,'" by Jerry Byrd; "Mexico," by Bob Moore. Still, Foster kept Monument's roster small and stressed quality. Because he spent so much time in Nashville, Foster in late 1959 moved his offices to suburban Hendersonville. He hired Byrd to oversee Combine Music. Monument's black paper record label with stark silver letters changed to a classy white with a Washington Monument logo.

"I was looking always for the unique artist, preferably one who wrote," Foster said. "Nashville was a little clannish in those days. The musicians' union was run with an iron hand by a guy named George Cooper. He wanted to make sure that anybody [producers] coming in to record was going to pay the bills. He didn't want any musicians being hung. Chet Atkins, who had carte blanche, helped me set up my first session. I guess having him approve of me didn't hurt. Then I went to Mr. Cooper and told him what I was doing. He said, 'We welcome the business. You just make sure you keep me paid.' And I did. I had one record and they accepted me. When Archie Bleyer wanted to come down to Nashville to cut the Everly Brothers, he had to put money with the union before he could come in. It wasn't the easiest thing in the world. I was the only label—or the only person—here in the music business who wasn't country. I hadn't even thought of cutting country records. I knew they weren't selling real well, so why bother. That got me on the outs with the local establishment. One of them asked me why I was ruining Nashville, what did I have against Nashville. He said I was polluting it and destroying it, and they had a good thing going here, and what did I mean by cutting all this bastard music, as he called it. I said, 'Look, there's only two kinds of music to me, good and bad, and I'm trying to be good.' "

The union musicians soon accepted Foster, and he used them regularly. He also hired new players trying to break into Nashville's closed-session ranks, such as guitarists Wayne Moss, Jerry Kennedy, later a producer for Mercury Records and Ray Edenton, a popular session man for years. Bass player Norburt Putnam, who later founded Quadrafonic Studios, played on Monument sessions, as did drummer Jerry Carrigan and arranger Bergen White. "I wanted to work the new guys in because I always try to be a little different," Foster said. "I wanted to make records that didn't sound like everything else. Monument had an identifiable sound, but different." In this quest, he signed writers Tony Joe White ("Polk Salad Annie"), Kristofferson, Arthur Alexander, Gatlin, Chris Gantry ("Dreams of the Everyday Housewife"), Bob Morrison ("Love the World Away"), and Dennis Linde, who wrote the Elvis Presley hit "Burning Love."

Combine became a respected Nashville publishing company.

To Foster, the singer and the song were inseparable, so he empha-sized song development. By the mid-1960s, he had hired former singer Bob Beckham to manage the Combine (BMI) and Music City (ASCAP) publishing companies. It proved fortunate, for Beckham's team wrote hits in pop, country, and R&B. Combine also acquired catalogs containing songs by such top country writers as Cindy Walker, Harlan Howard, and Jimmy Driftwood. Combine also ad-ministered Rising Sons Music, the publishing firm started by Bobby Russell and Buzz Cason.

Despite Foster's impressive song catalog, he refused to record his own material exclusively. In fact, Combine writers had to lobby for their material. Foster was interested in good songs, regardless of who owned them. At the time, Nashville labels and producers rou-tinely recorded their own property. Foster concentrated intensely on a song and learned its inner workings, especially in the studio. "In some intuitive way," songwriter Boudeleaux Bryant once said of his fishing buddy, "he seems to be able to cut through the morass of sound that fills the studio control room and to hear with some extraordinary faculty just what is wrong, or right, with the perfor-mance of a huge room full of musicians." [2]

This intuition paid off when Orbison joined Monument in 1960. Although his first two singles on the label failed to sell, Foster felt goosebumps when he heard Orbison's falsetto voice, and he was equally impressed with the singer's melodies. At Foster's suggestion, Orbison combined two original songs into "Only the Lonely (Know the Way I Feel)," now a landmark American pop song. The Foster/Orbison team clicked, personally and professionally.

Perhaps Foster's relaxed personality allowed the shy Orbison to express himself in the studio. "Roy Orbison used to hang around the studio showing his songs to recording artists," Bryant said. "I remem-ber him as a timid, shy kid who seemed to be rather befuddled by the whole music scene. I remember the way he sang them – softly, prettily, but also as if afraid someone might be disturbed by his efforts and reprimand him. Then he was signed by Monument Records, and a transformation occurred." [3]

Foster produced nearly all of Orbison's Monument releases,

146

which are now classics: "Blue Angel," 1960; "Running Scared" and "Crying," 1961; "Dream Baby (How Long Must I Dream)," 1962; "Mean Woman Blues," "In Dreams," and "Blue Bayou," 1963; "Oh, Pretty Woman" and "It's Over," 1964. They came when successive hits were difficult to break, especially for American singers with 1950s hairstyles in a market infiltrated by mop-haired British acts. At the time, most of Orbison's rockabilly contemporaries from the mid-1950s were struggling or out of the music business. But Foster kept Orbison on top, skillfully mixing his original songs with outside material.

The Foster/Orbison team was coasting on the charts when Orbison's manager, Wesley Rose, tried to transform the bespectacled Orbison into a bigger act after his Monument contract expired in June 1965. It was a disastrous move. "Wesley Rose decided he wanted to move Roy for a million dollars, a movie contract, and guaranteed TV appearances," Foster said. "I said, 'Well, I can give the million dollars, but I can't guarantee you a movie deal because I don't own a studio.' "

Orbison ultimately signed his first million-dollar contract with MGM. He owed Monument four more sides, but Rose attempted to dictate to Foster what songs would be released and when. "So I said, 'Then *you* do it [produce the records]', " said Foster. "So we went from selling seven million copies on 'Oh Pretty Woman' to less than 200,000 on the follow-up. It broke my heart. The next one didn't even break 100,000. That should have been the writing on the wall. I mean, a million dollars is nice, but if you can stay where you are and keep rolling, a million dollars is nothing. You make more than that anyway. But that's the way it came down."[4]

Foster regretted losing Orbison to MGM, and, in 1988, to death at age 52. Orbison joined MGM with visions of greater success but never appeared in the national top 10 again until 1988, with the collaborative Traveling Wilburys album. He died in December of that year. Some critics contend that Orbison never found another producer with Foster's touch. Foster believes that they had a special collaborative spirit together that could not be recaptured. Perhaps Foster's dual roles of producer and label president enabled the team

Roy Orbison was a struggling singer and songwriter until he joined Fred Foster's little-known Monument label in 1960 in Nashville. Foster brilliantly showcased the unique voice of Orbison, who recorded a series of rock 'n' roll hits for the young record company.

Little Labels—Big Sound

to excel. Because he controlled session budgets, for example, he allowed Orbison an incredible 36 takes on "It's Over." By the time Rose produced Orbison's final Monument singles, "Goodnight" and "(Say) You're My Girl," the spark was gone.

After years of rehashing his old sound, Orbison returned to Monument in 1977 with an album, *Regeneration*, which Foster produced. Foster sought a fresher, hip sound, using material from some of Nashville's and Combine's top writers, including Dennis Linde and Kristofferson. It was a dark period for Orbison, who had endured personal tragedies. He did not write one song on the album. In trade advertisements, Foster thanked Wesley Rose and called *Regeneration* "a rebirth of the magic and the music we thank God for. Personally and professionally our relationship is rekindled and renewed. Now the Golden Years are all ahead." Despite accompaniment by top Nashville session players, the album flopped. Orbison asked to be released from his contract. Foster complied, knowing the magic was lost forever. Soon after, Orbison began experiencing heart trouble.

Orbison's original departure from Monument in 1965 could have been a fatal loss to many independent labels. But during Orbison's reign, Foster and his team never stopped discovering offbeat artists. Before Orbison, Monument was a singles label that survived on one-hit or two-hit artists. But as Monument grew from 1960 to 1975, Foster used the enormous income from Orbison's string of hits to expand his record and publishing companies, open a Hollywood office, buy a Nashville recording studio, and hire experienced managers. By the late 1960s, Monument's performers sold albums as well as singles. Boots Randolph, Monument's all-time sales leader, never dominated the singles chart, but his 1963 hit single, "Yakety Sax," launched a series of albums that sold millions.

Also in 1963, Foster pursued the R&B market with a new subsidiary, Sound Stage 7 Records, which was launched with the hits "(Down at) Papa Joe's" and "Southtown, U.S.A." by the Dixiebelles. Foster created Sound Stage 7 after disc jockeys refused to play an R&B record on Monument. "I was bombarded with letters, telephone calls, and telegrams, asking me what I was trying to do," he

149

said. "As it turned out, a lot of jocks would put a Monument record on the air without auditioning it. Some of these country guys – well, not really country; 'chicken rock,' I call them–played low-profile music, and suddenly they put on this screaming R&B record. Their phones lighted up. People wanted to know what was going on. So I said I would create a label for R&B, so the jocks would know. I just picked the name Sound Stage 7 out of the air."

John Richbourg, a white Nashville disc jockey who played black music on WLAC, asked to work with the label. He became the A&R manager, but Foster retained ultimate control. "He played Joe Simon's 'The Chokin' Kind' for me," Foster said. "I said, 'I think you need to remix it. The bass is way too hot.' John R. said, 'Fred, I mixed it that way on purpose. That's the way I want it.' Now, I had the right to overrule him, of course, but I didn't. He was right and I was wrong." Simon's version of the country hit "The Chokin' Kind" earned him a gold record in 1969. From 1966-1970, his singles hit the pop charts 14 times and were fixtures on national R&B charts.

Monument by the 1960s focused on country records and signed Grandpa Jones, a country star with King Records in the mid-1940s. By 1960s standards, Jones was old-fashioned, but Foster produced some fine albums for him. "Of all my records on many different labels," Jones said, " the best are the ones I did for Monument. Fred Foster was a big part of that. You have to give him credit. He kept putting singles out on me, even though I was never what you'd call a real singles artist." [5] Except for "T for Texas," a top five country hit in 1962, Grandpa's singles failed to sell. But Foster never considered decreasing Grandpa's releases. Foster enjoyed his humor and intelligence, and believed in him as an artist. "I just let Grandpa be himself," Foster said. "I never did try to 'produce' him. I tried to make the surroundings as agreeable as possible. We made some fine albums."

In 1965, Foster also signed a talented songwriter with an odd voice named Dolly Parton. She had no success with other record companies, but Foster heard something soulful in that Appalachian twang. Foster signed her to a Monument artist's contract as well as a Combine Music writer's contract. Wayne Moss recalled: "Fred used

Little Labels — Big Sound

to bring Dolly into the studio to record some rhythm and blues songs because she sounded good on them. She'd finish singing and turn to us in the studio and say, 'Well, fellas, how'd y'all think that sounded, anyway?' " [6] Foster invested $50,000 to build her career, which began to rise when she teamed up with country male singer Porter Wagoner. Foster finally cut a country hit for Parton in 1966, with Curly Putnam's song "Dumb Blonde." However, Parton soon joined RCA Records leaving Foster with 24 sides recorded by her and a feeling of frustration for what might have been.

In the late 1960s, Foster encouraged comic singer Ray Stevens to write serious material. The *Even Stevens* album, including "Unwind" and "Mr. Businessman," returned Stevens to the charts after a two-year absence. Then, he and Foster returned to the novelty genre with the forgettable singles "Gitarzan" and "Along Came Jones." Foster produced an obscure album, *Introspection*, for singer-songwriter Chris Gantry. His single, "Dreams of the Everyday Housewife," was not a hit, but it had a distinct energy that Glen Campbell's hit version lacked. An eccentric writer and erratic singer, Gantry was a typical Fred Foster artist.

By this stage, Foster seemed enamored with offbeat songwriters, including Tony Joe White, a deep-voiced singer schooled in the blues. White's vocals were powerful, and his songs were snapshots of his Southern life. His music attracted Combine staff writer Billy Swan, who wanted to produce an album for the white Louisiana native. On White's first album, *Black and White*, Swan hired white soul musicians for sessions in Nashville and Memphis. With its humorous lyrics and perky Bergen White horn arrangement, "Polk Salad Annie" stood out from the other album cuts. Foster loved White's music, but he didn't know Atlantic Records did, too. As Foster explained it:

> There was an engineer in Memphis who sent taped copies of our sessions to Jerry Wexler at Atlantic. He had them before I did. So almost from day one, Atlantic wanted Tony Joe. The reason I found out is that we didn't have an album out with the song "Willie and Laura Mae Jones," and Dusty Springfield cut

151

it for Atlantic. I said, "How did Dusty Springfield get the song?" We could not have licensed it, of course, but Tony Joe came to me all excited and said, "Miss Dusty Springfield is cutting my next single!"

We were planning that song as his next single, you see, and we just hadn't been able to break "Polk Salad Annie" [White's previous single]. It would flurry a little in New Orleans, then a little in Chicago, Baltimore, San Francisco. But if I ever heard a record that I thought was a hit, that was it. I knew something was wrong. It had to be the timing. Or we said maybe the record is so different that we'll just have to keep going until people realize what it is. When Dusty Springfield's release of "Willie and Laura Mae Jones" was only three weeks away, Tony Joe came to me and asked what we were going to do. I said we could stick with "Polk Salad Annie" or drop it and release his version of "Willie and Laura Mae Jones" tomorrow. I could have put it out in 24 hours. I said, "Let me sleep on it. Call me in the morning." So he called me and said, "What are we doing?" I said, "We're sticking with 'Polk Salad.'" He said, "Well, it's only my career. I'm glad you're the one who had to make the decision."

I called our promo guys and said, "Whoever succeeds in breaking this record, you'll never be sorry." The L.A. promotion man broke it two months later. He was just getting married. I said, "Where are you going on your honeymoon?" He said, "We can't afford to go anywhere. We'll probably drive up to San Francisco." I said, "Where would you like to go?" He said, "Hawaii." So I sent the couple to Hawaii and paid all their expenses. "Polk Salad" became a huge hit for us.

The record, with its blaring horns and bluesy guitar, was typical of what Tony Joe called swamp music—funky songs with rural themes and soulful vocals. Two more Monument albums followed. "Atlantic was really all over us, watching everything," Foster said. "His [White's] follow-up to 'Polk Salad'—'Roosevelt and Ira Lee'—was good, but I didn't think it was quite different enough and strong enough to become a great hit. We had nothing else, though. And I told Tony Joe that. It was a mistake to put it out. You should never do

Little Labels—Big Sound

that." In three years, Monument lost White to Warner Brothers, but White never regained his success on the singles charts.

White's success on Monument foreshadowed the arrival of the ultimate Fosteresque singer, Kris Kristofferson, for whom Foster produced several albums and singles in the early 1970s, including the million-seller "Why Me." Foster remembered the first time he heard Kristofferson: "Bob Beckham called and said he had a guy who wanted to move from another publisher to Combine, but he wanted a little more money than our usual writer's figure. Bob brought Kris out to see me. He played a few of his songs and I thought that Kris was a singer who didn't sound like everyone else. I said, 'I'll sign you as a writer on one condition: You'll agree to do an album for Monument.' He said, 'You've got to be crazy.' I said, 'Maybe, but that's what I want.' Kris said, 'If you're crazy enough, I'm crazy enough.' "

Gravelly-voiced, soulful, and original, Kristofferson was a Rhodes scholar who wrote "Help Me Make It Through the Night" for Sammi Smith and "For the Good Times" for Ray Price. He soon developed a following with his own Monument albums. Foster called him the poet of his time. Of all Foster's important productions over the decades, Kristofferson's "Casey's Last Ride" became one of his favorites. "Here was an artist who was unusual," Foster said. "I wanted him for Monument. I had passed up a lot of great singers because they weren't unique. Knowing this, somebody said to me, 'How could you sign Kristofferson? He can't sing.' I said, 'No, but he can communicate.' He sold me. And he doesn't sound like anybody. Johnny Cash, Willie Nelson, Dolly Parton, Roy Orbison. They don't sound like anybody, either."

By the early 1970s, however, Foster realized that no matter how different his artists were, they were not being heard by enough people. Monument's independent distribution lacked the muscle to sell millions of records quickly. Clive Davis, head of Columbia Records, wanted to be involved in Kristofferson's career, but Foster resisted. So Davis offered to distribute Monument nationally to get Kristofferson. Foster accepted, and Monument received a new company logo—monuments arranged to resemble something like a peace symbol – and the clout of America's most powerful record company.

153

Veteran writer Swan provided the label with a million-seller in "I Can Help." By 1977, Monument received another logo change—its name written in stones—and a new distribution agreement with another worldwide record power, Phonogram.

"Monument was always independent," Foster said, "but in those days you had to have other distribution because the independent distributors were so much trouble. They weren't paying their bills. Through the independents, I managed to sell a grand total of 35,000 copies of the first Kristofferson album. When the Columbia [distribution] deal started, I had just finished his second album, *Silver-Tongued Devil*. It went gold in two to three weeks. They re-released the first album and it went gold in about a month. It was unbelievable, the power they had. The whole Monument catalog just started resurging."

In 1981, Foster and Monument were poised for another successful decade. Foster had become wealthy from his recordings, so a friend asked him to buy a huge block of stock in his Nashville bank. Foster was to hold the stock only six months. Then, without warning, the bank failed. "I lost a ton of money," Foster said. "One thing led to another until I had to sell my assets. I never would have invested in the bank if I had had any brains, but I thought I was helping a friend." Foster sold Monument to Sony/Columbia and Combine Music to entrepreneur Charles Koppelman and SBK Records, which then sold Combine's catalog to EMI Records.

In the late 1990s, Sony reactivated Monument. In 1994, Sony released a double compact disc, *The Monument Story*, featuring Foster's brief history of the recordings and the company. By then, the semiretired Foster was living in a fashionable Nashville neighborhood and producing records for other labels through his production company, Sunstone. He still sought writers and singers who sounded different, who gave him the same goosebumps he felt when he first heard Orbison.

"I look back on it all, on forming the label, and I think it was just something I had to do," he said. "I never did promote drugs, drinking, promiscuous sex, or anything like that. I always wanted my children to be able to listen to the records and be proud of them. I had a

Little Labels—Big Sound

philosophy, and I wish more people would adopt it: For me to get heard, I had to make a better record than anything that's out there. I didn't always succeed; maybe never, I don't know. But I tried. I never thought about making money. I was a fan first. I only wanted to make the best possible music I could make, and I figured the rest would take care of itself."

delmark

Stereo   DS-647-B

NORTH/ /SOUTH
THE JIMMY JOHNSON BAND

1. Talking 'Bout Chicago   (4:45)
2. A Woman Ain't Supposed To Be Hard   (4:32)
3. I Can't Survive   (3:47)
4. Sang A Song In Heaven   (2:56)
5. Dead Or Alive   (4:43)

all songs by Jimmy Johnson
© 1982 Granite City Music—BMI
DELMARK RECORDS
4243 N. Lincoln—Chicago, IL

(41075)
℗ 1982

Ten / **Delmark Records**

"Sometimes you put wonderful records out there, such
as 'Hoodoo Man Blues,' but the world isn't ready for
them just yet."

—Bob Koester, Delmark Records owner

In late 1969, Bruce Iglauer turned up at Bob Koester's downtown Chicago record store to immerse himself in the city's blues scene. The Jazz Record Mart, on a seedy strip of West Grand Avenue, was a hangout for jazz and blues musicians and aficionados. Modest in decor, the store was packed with hard-to-find records. But the main attraction was the 37-year-old Koester, an eccentric, opinionated, and tireless promoter of Chicago jazz and blues who was known to close the store at night and take customers to the neighborhood black clubs.

Koester also operated his own Delmark Records, which had a small, loyal following for its influential jazz and blues records. The 22-year-old Iglauer, a child of the 1960s blues and folk revival who promoted blues acts in college, jumped at the chance to work for $30 a week as a Delmark shipping clerk and store assistant. "The Jazz Record Mart was a magical gateway between pure Chicago black ghetto blues and the international network of us white fans," Iglauer recalled. "Bob [Koester] didn't have a racist bone in his body, and the black musicians respected him for that. He'd be in clubs where he might be the only white guy and wouldn't think anything of it. Through Bob, I wanted to get an inside track on the music." [1]

Iglauer soon got his wish. During a blizzard in early 1970, Koester organized a Delmark recording session for a local blues harmonica player, Junior Wells, with a band that included guitarist Buddy Guy and pianist Otis Spann. Before they could start, Iglauer raced across town to bail the drummer out of jail following a traffic violation. Wells, who in 1965 recorded the now-classic "Hoodoo Man Blues" album for Delmark, arrived for the session with no song list. So, Spann, a longtime Chicago blues fixture who performed for years with Muddy Waters, called out songs from the piano.

"Junior didn't always know all the words, so he just made them up," Iglauer recalled. "On the song 'Lend Me Your Love,' he made up words with that special Junior stream of consciousness, which was just incredible. Otis Spann would suggest another song, and off they went. Later on, I saw Bob edit the tape [from the session], using a razor blade, right there on his living room table. It became the record

Robert Koester, founder and owner of the Delmark label, at his Jazz Record Mart store in Chicago. Koester is a throwback to an earlier era, when tiny but influential jazz labels operated out of neighborhood music stores.

Little Labels—Big Sound

'Southside Blues Jam.' I was amazed at how his Delmark operation was so homegrown and personal."

Working for the volatile Koester, Iglauer received the internship of a lifetime. Within a few years, Iglauer left to form Alligator Records, the most successful blues label since the 1970s and a catalyst for the 1980s blues revival. He became one of several graduates from Koester's operation to make his own mark on the blues and jazz world, along with Chuck Nessa of Nessa Records, Michael Frank of Earwig Records, and Jim O'Neal of Rooster Blues Records, who also co-founded *Living Blues* magazine after posting a sign-up sheet in The Jazz Record Mart.

Today, Chicago's blues scene is far more commercially viable, with a worldwide draw. The city's upscale blues clubs are tourist spots and its annual blues festival has attracted millions of people. Koester played a major role in this transformation. While Chess Records, and later Alligator Records, have been Chicago's dominant blues labels, Koester's Delmark label and the Jazz Record Mart have advanced Chicago blues at the grassroots level for more than 30 years.

"Without Bob, there would have never been the white following we have today for blues music," said Iglauer. "In the 1960s, Bob Koester was putting out black ghetto music on Delmark at a time when there wasn't an audience for it." In the mid-1960s, Delmark pioneered the modern blues album and captured on vinyl Chicago's explosive club scene. It created a ground swell. "What Bob was doing was basically unheard of in the mid-1960s," said Iglauer. "He was a radical and a visionary."

Since the 1950s, Koester has run Delmark with a fiery passion for undiluted jazz and blues, and with a deaf ear toward trendy music. Essentially, Delmark served a small commercial base by design. In the late 1950s and early 1960s, when jazz labels embraced the "cool jazz" sound popularized by Dave Brubeck, Chet Baker, and Miles Davis, Koester recorded the traditional jazz he felt was neglected. At the same time, Koester revitalized the careers of aging country blues singers Sleepy John Estes, Big Joe Williams, Arthur Crudup, Yank Rachell, and Roosevelt Sykes. In the late 1960s, Delmark introduced the world to Chicago's radical, freeform jazz movement, with break-

Delmark Records

through albums featuring Roscoe Mitchell, Lester Bowie, Anthony Braxton, Muhal Richard Abrams, Joseph Jarman, and the Art Ensemble of Chicago. And for decades, Delmark has been a driving force behind the documentation of contemporary Chicago blues musicians by issuing important records by Wells, Magic Sam, Otis Rush, Robert Jr. Lockwood, Luther Allison, Jimmy Johnson, and numerous others.

Today, Delmark's output is at a high. The label wins the critics' accolades for its current blues and jazz lineup, which continues to capture Chicago's musical pulse. In addition to reissuing original Delmark classics, Koester has put back into circulation recordings from long-defunct labels, such as Apollo. With much of its 40-year record catalog still in print, Delmark is grounded in longevity. "The whole idea with Delmark has never been to have a hit record, but to sell the records over many, many years," Koester said. "You don't sell much right out of the box [with jazz and blues], but you can sell the records in small amounts forever."[2]

For most years, Koester has operated Delmark through the cash register of his Jazz Record Mart, a Chicago institution. The label and the store have natural synergy. "The record store and record label combination is a tradition going back to the 1930s with Milt Gabler's Commodore Music Store and Commodore label in Manhattan, or Ross Russell's Los Angeles music store and Dial label in the 1940s," Koester said. "There were years when I put out only a handful of [Delmark] records, so the store kept the whole thing going."

Before moving the store in 1995 to a larger facility on Wabash Avenue, Koester had operated the Jazz Record Mart since 1962 on West Grand Avenue, west of the Chicago's "Loop." At both places, the store's inventory has been legendary, with some records available nowhere else. Leading blues, jazz, and rock musicians have long been store regulars. In the 1960s, blues singer Big Joe Williams slept on a cot in the store's cellar when performing in Chicago. Wells once had his own store key. "I remember getting into a horrible shouting match with [blues guitarist] Michael Bloomfield over the subject of modern jazz while I was working behind the cash register," recalled record producer Chuck Nessa, a Jazz Record Mart employee in the mid-1960s. "The most incredible musicians would walk through the door." [3]

Considering Koester's first commercial venture in records as a teenager involved buying, selling, and trading jazz and blues 78-rpm discs, the Jazz Record Mart, appropriately, sells vintage 78-rpm discs, right along with vinyl albums and CDs. A walking encyclopedia on the music, Koester never hesitates to offer an opinion to customers, or even argue with them over the counter. It is part of his nature. Since childhood, Koester has been wildly passionate about blues and jazz, and his brash enthusiasm has rubbed off on listeners worldwide.

"I was in the polio ward during the sixth grade for about three or four months," said Koester, born in 1932, the son of a petroleum geologist in Wichita, Kansas. "This was around 1943–44, the war years. I listened to the radio all day, and I always spruced up when I heard Benny Goodman or Eddie Condon, as opposed to something by Perry Como. That's basically where it really started for me. By the time I was a teenager, I was a jazz fanatic. I was very catholic in my tastes — big bands, boogie-woogie music. As I started buying old jazz records in the Salvation Army store, I soon realized that black music was the hippest. Over time, I broadened my interests to include music categorized as black blues. But to me, Blind Boy Fuller and Memphis Minnie were as much a part of jazz as Charlie Parker. I was not aware of a distinction."

A small town in the Kansas plains, Wichita in the late 1940s was no jazz hotbed. But the young Koester pursued bands passing through town and those based a few hours away in Kansas City, Missouri, a vibrant jazz city since Prohibition. "I begged my parents to see Red Allen, and I remember hearing Count Basie with Jimmy Rushing as his singer," Koester recalled. "In Kansas City, of course, you had the great pianist Jay McShann. I was inspired by an alto saxophonist who recorded with McShann named Tommy Douglas. I went to see Lionel Hampton at what they called a 'colored dance.' The whites had to sit in the balcony, but later, you could join in on the dance floor. There was a kid at our Catholic high school, one of only three black kids in the school, whose uncle was in the Basie band. All of these things added up to make an impression."

161

Even beyond his passion for black music, Koester was not a typical Kansas kid. An aviation enthusiast, he rode his bicycle to the local airport to dust off the airplanes. He sold Christmas cards door-to-door and used the commissions to buy a primitive movie camera, which fostered a lifelong fascination with film. (Three of his four brothers eventually worked in the film industry.) "In high school, I was considered a little strange," Koester said laughing. "Why did I want to carry a football? You could get hurt. The word sissy was used. But I was very much an entrepreneur, particularly when I got to college."

From his dormitory room at St. Louis University, Koester sold 78-rpm jazz and blues discs through record collector magazines. In his sophomore year, he opened the Blue Note Record Shop in a tiny storefront, formerly a barbecue pit, near the campus along Delmar Boulevard, a main thoroughfare running west of the Mississippi River through downtown St. Louis. Koester sold music collector items, such as hard-to-find Dixieland classics and reissued Paramount blues and jazz records. "I had a friend who sold bebop records, so we combined our resources and bought Commodore and Blue Note releases out of New York," Koester said. "He [the friend] took the bebop records and I took the traditional jazz stuff."

The enterprise gradually consumed him. The store opened at night, but it became Koester's daytime refuge. He was known to sleep at the counter between classes. When he dropped out of college as a junior ("accounting killed me"), Koester made retailing in jazz music his main occupation, along with various odd jobs. This infuriated his father, who "had visions of me becoming a junkie," Koester said. (He did manage to get arrested for selling liquor to a minor in a local club.) Between 1953 and 1958, Koester was a fixture on Delmar Boulevard, and in the neighborhood clubs. Much to Koester's liking, St. Louis still featured a half-dozen nightspots with traditional jazz bands, despite a youth-led bebop movement that put older jazz players out of work around the country.

Financed by a local jazz promoter named John Galbraith, Koester organized his first recording session, in September 1953, for a traditional jazz band, The Fabulous Windy City Six, fronted by

Little Labels—Big Sound

horn player Sammy Gardner. The session was held in the basement studio of a local architecture professor. Koester was just 22 years old when he pressed 486 copies of a 10-inch record from the session, for his own label, called Delmar (the "k" was added later), which was named after the well-known St. Louis street. "Bob was wrapped up in the blues and jazz aspects of St. Louis and with some of the early figures in the music who were still around town," recalled Frank Powers, a longtime jazz musician who visited Koester's store in the mid-1950s on a weekend pass from the military. "His store was tiny, but there was always something going on, people staying there, musicians dropping by. Bob had a special feeling for the local musical heritage and put some of these guys on the Delmar label." [4]

Speckled Red (Rufus Perryman) and Big Joe Williams, two longtime blues performers in St. Louis in the mid-1950s, brought attention to Koester's label. An albino black boogie-woogie piano player, Speckled Red recorded "The Dirty Dozens" for the Brunswick label in 1929 and recorded sides during the Depression for the Bluebird label. In the 1950s, with his early records desired by collectors, Speckled Red was scratching out a living by playing in St. Louis bars. Koester produced several sides for him in what amounted to an "artist rediscovery." (This material is now compiled on a Delmark CD titled "The Dirty Dozens.") The exposure from Koester's little label helped Speckled Red to land record deals with other independent labels and tour dates in America and Europe in the late 1950s.

Big Joe Williams, a raspy-voiced Mississippi Delta blues singer and guitarist, had been a smalltime traveling act for decades when he met Koester. In addition to performing with the Delta's blues pioneers, Williams recorded for Bluebird in the 1930s and 1940s. Frequently in St. Louis in the 1950s, Williams recorded for Koester on a straight cash deal. "He [Williams] would live in St. Louis with relatives for a few months until they would get fed up with him and kick him out," Koester said. "I paid him $10 or $20 for each session and recorded him in the record store. Unlike Speckled Red, he never got drunk for sessions. He was a hell of an artist and gave the label distinction." Over time, Koester produced several albums for Williams, including the classic 1958 album "Starvin' Chain Blues," with

163

Williams' cousin, J. D. Short, another Delta blues shouter, who was living in St. Louis.

Koester made modest inroads in St. Louis with Delmar by recording area musicians, and by reissuing masters by George Lewis' New Orleans Jazz Band. In 1956, Koester issued the first Delmar album, featuring a traditional jazz band called The Dixie Stompers. But faced with record discounting from area competitors and encouraged by John Steiner, owner of the Paramount catalog, to "get going young man," Koester moved to Chicago in August 1958. A Delmar distributor in Chicago provided some seed money for Koester's hand-to-mouth record business. Within a year, Koester purchased Seymour's Jazz Record Mart on South Wabash Avenue for $1,500. "What I bought of value was an ancient cash register," recalled Koester, who operated Seymour's from 1959 to 1962.

During that period, Koester's own record catalog slowly expanded. Koester produced jazz pianist Art Hodes, trumpeter Ira Sullivan, and saxophonist Jimmy Forrest, who was backed by members of the Harry Edison Orchestra. Koester issued his first modern jazz record with an album by a band led by Bob Graf. When Big Joe Williams needed money to buy burial benefits from a lodge (Williams died in 1982 at age 79), Koester paid him $20 to record several masters ultimately released on Folkways Records. Around this time, a European instrument manufacturer objected to the use of the Delmar name, and Koester added the "k" to form Delmark.

Delmark also promoted the country blues and folk revival of the early 1960s, when young fans searched for the forgotten black blues singers who recorded in the 1920s and 1930s. In 1962, Koester learned the whereabouts of blues singer Sleepy John Estes, a blind guitarist and singer living in poverty in Tennessee. Estes had recorded for Victor, Decca, and Bluebird during the Depression. By the 1950s, many blues aficionados thought he was dead. Koester heard tapes from an Estes film documentary and brought him to Chicago. Over the next three years, Koester produced four albums for Estes, including the notable "Broke and Hungry" in 1964. On this session, Koester teamed Estes with longtime collaborators Hammie Nixon on harmonica and Yank Rachell on mandolin. The white blues guitarist Michael Bloomfield joined Estes on several tracks. "In a strange coincidence, there was a clothing store next to Seymour's called the Davis Congress Shop, where this old guy named Sam worked," Koester said. "When John [Estes] got to town, I asked him where he wanted to go. He said to visit his brother, Sam Estes, who worked right next door."

In late 1962, Koester moved his store to West Grand Avenue. He renamed it "The Jazz Record Mart," which, he said, "moved it up the alphabet in the Yellow Pages." It became his base of operation for more than 30 years. "West Grand Avenue during this time was basically a slum," he said. "At first glance, I thought the place was terrible, but the real estate agent said it was good. The building had a dusty veneer that was great. Early on, I sold records to the prostitutes who worked the neighborhood."

As was his habit, Koester absorbed the local music scene, frequenting the blues nightspots of the ghetto. An encounter in the now-historic Theresa's Lounge led Koester in 1965 to record Junior Wells and Buddy Guy on one of the first and greatest Chicago blues albums, "Hoodoo Man Blues." A native of Memphis, Tennessee, Wells had performed in Chicago since the 1940s, including a stint on harmonica with Muddy Waters. Around 1958, Wells began performing in local clubs with Guy, a guitarist, who had moved to Chicago the previous year from his native Louisiana. By the early 1960s, Wells had modestly selling releases on the small Profile and Chief labels. Meanwhile, Guy backed Chess artists and recorded sides on the label under his own name, but both men essentially remained local attractions.

Koester, familiar with Wells' records on Chief, was struck by his energy and distinctive vocals as he fronted Theresa's house band. Koester proposed a recording session. Wells refused an exclusive arrangement, so Koester offered to pay slightly over union scale for the session, plus 5 percent royalties on sales. Guy joined the session, but, believing he was still under contract with Chess, instructed Koester to obtain permission from label owner Leonard Chess. "Leonard told me not to use Guy's name on the album, even though I found out later that Guy was not under contract with Chess at the time," Koester said. Guy was billed "the friendly chap" on the initial album releases.

Issued in early 1966, the raw, blatantly non-commercial "Hoodoo Man Blues" put the world on notice that Chicago blues, though grounded in the old Mississippi Delta tradition, was not museum music. On the contrary, it was a living and vibrant sound that proved well-suited for the album format. Powered by Wells' rich voice and Guy's biting guitar fills, "Hoodoo Man Blues" has sold more than 100,000 copies since 1966 and grows in stature yearly as record reviewers praise its unrestrained passion. As blues writer Bill Dahl wrote recently, the album is "one of the truly classic blues albums of the 1960s and one of the first to document the smoky ambiance of a night at a Westside night spot in the superior acoustic of a recording studio." [5]

"Hoodoo Man Blues" jump-started Wells' career by creating an audience apart from Chicago's ghetto clubs. He soon signed with the Mercury label, and later, Vanguard, which prevented Koester from producing a follow-up album. However, Wells and Koester remained close and eventually recorded two more albums together, including the classic "Southside Blues Jam." As Koester recalled: "I would see Junior all over town. One night in the late 1960s, I got in a limousine with Junior on the way to a gig and I agreed to pay double scale for his next session for Delmark. But two years passed and nothing happened. I finally hooked up with Junior again in a club and suggested we work a deal, but Junior said we already worked out a deal in the limousine two years before. This led to the 'Southside Blues Jam' session. That was typical of Junior's integrity. I was glad to make three albums with him."

During the period, Delmark also recorded a phenomenal west side blues guitarist named Sam Maghatt, who performed as "Magic Sam." A Mississippi Delta native, Magic Sam also recorded for Chief in the early 1960s and was a regular in Chicago's black blues clubs, such as Sylvio's. An energetic singer, Magic Sam also played driving solos reminiscent of Jimi Hendrix. In 1968, Magic Sam recorded his only studio album, Delmark's "West Side Soul," which, like "Hoodoo Man Blues," has become a modern blues classic. "Magic Sam Live,"

HOODOO MAN BLUES 🔲
JUNIOR WELLS'
CHICAGO BLUES BAND
with BUDDY GUY

Junior Wells' 1966 album "Hoodoo Man Blues" on Delmark was among the first modern Chicago blues albums ever issued. It is now universally regarded as a blues classic.

originally issued on Delmark as a double album, captures a sizzling performance at the 1969 Ann Arbor, Michigan, Blues Festival. (At the same festival, Koester also struck a deal with blues singer Robert Jr. Lockwood, nephew of Delta legend Robert Johnson, which led to Lockwood recording the album "Steady Rollin' Man" on Delmark.) Shortly after the Ann Arbor festival, Magic Sam died at the height of his powers at age 32.

167

Delmark Records

Fortunately, Koester had taped hours of live and studio performances, representing the lion's share of Magic Sam's recorded output. Koester has remastered and released Magic Sam's Delmark masters on CDs, including several previously unissued songs and portions of a 1968 rehearsal. "He [Magic Sam] was such a sweet, happy-go-lucky kind of guy," Koester said. "He was very family oriented, and loved to have rib roasts in his backyard. Whenever he came into some serious money, he bought ribs. He didn't realize he had a serious heart condition and he should have slowed down. Just a wonderful man."

While Koester made history with Wells and Magic Sam, Delmark also became a significant jazz label. The Association for the Advancement of Creative Musicians (AACM), a Chicago music cooperative of black musicians playing free-form jazz, added new textures to the jazz landscape with modestly selling, but inspiring, Delmark releases. The collaboration began in 1966 when Koester, always the mentor, allowed store employee Chuck Nessa to produce jazz albums for Delmark. "Here I was, just this Iowa college kid and new to Chicago, and Koester is letting me produce the jazz music of my choosing," Nessa recalled. "Koester really didn't have the money to do this, but he agreed to let me produce three records. I began searching Chicago for jazz, which led me to the AACM guys."

The AACM was formed in 1965 by established pianist Muhal Richard Abrams and other lesser-known musicians. Because their freeform style of jazz had no commercial outlet, AACM members pulled together and found places to perform their work. They also organized a music school. Strong African-American pride and discipline within AACM gave the young musicians a powerful sense of direction. In 1966, Nessa heard AACM saxophonist Roscoe Mitchell, then 22, and proposed a record deal for his sextet, which included trumpeter Lester Bowie and bassist Malachi Favors. While fascinated by their approach to playing jazz, the inexperienced Nessa found recording them another matter. "Musically, it was a very unpredictable group, and as their so-called producer, I didn't know what the hell I was doing," Nessa said. "I simply told the sound engineer what I thought they would sound like, such as when they

Recording for Delmark in the late 1960s, avant-garde saxophonist Roscoe Mitchell greatly influenced the free jazz movement. His 1966 Delmark recording "Sound" has become part of the jazz record canon.

might get loud or soft. It was maddening at first, but proved to be a very exciting experience."

The resulting Delmark release, "Sound," sold few copies, but it inspired other AACM members. The organized, collective improvisation on Mitchell's "Sound" was marked by soft tones and stretches of silence. "Sound" contrasted the free jazz of the East Coast, most notably the density of sound from saxophonist John Coltrane. Years passed before "Sound" influenced audiences outside of Chicago, but as with many Delmark projects, time was on its side. Nessa's second Delmark production, "Song For," featured a group led by the AACM's Joseph Jarman, a reed player recommended to Nessa by Mitchell. In early 1967, Nessa produced his third Delmark album, "Level of Degrees of Light" by Abrams, with then-unknown saxophonist Anthony Braxton.

No jazz albums had ever sounded like these Delmark projects. Their limited distribution did not prevent jazz critics from raving. Nessa was onto something and Koester knew it. "Initially, I wasn't wild about it ["Sound"], but I could hear immense creativity," said Koester. "When *Downbeat* magazine gave the album a five-star rating, I thought this was interesting." Koester was not directly involved in the first AACM sessions, and recalled the members were "into the angry black thing." Still, he seized the opportunity to make an important contribution to jazz. "I figured I'm never going to find a Jelly Roll Morton or Duke Ellington or Johnny Hodges," he said. "But I realized that if I would ever find someone on that creative level, I probably wouldn't dig the music. Maybe I didn't understand what they [the AACM members] were doing, but I was sure they would be important to jazz history. The 'Sound' album was a major move in a new direction for Delmark, and for jazz."

Within a year of the "Sound" recording session, Nessa's relationship with his boss deteriorated. He left Koester's employment and formed Nessa Records. The small label, described by its founder as more of a "record boutique," produced several milestone records by AACM members in the 1960s and early 1970s, most notably the debut album by the Art Ensemble of Chicago, a landmark group formed in 1971 by AACM members Mitchell, Favors, Bowie, and

Jarman. Without Nessa's enthusiasm and Koester's initial financial support for the early AACM recordings, the Art Ensemble of Chicago may have never been launched as a commercially viable band.

Freeform jazz continued at Delmark after Nessa's departure when Abrams recommended Anthony Braxton for a session. As the 1960s drew to a close, Koester produced two albums for Braxton, "3 Compositions in New Jazz" and "For Alto." The later release, an ambitious double album issued in 1971, with Braxton, unaccompanied, on the alto saxophone, celebrated the AACM creative spirit, launched Braxton's solo career, and contributed to a brief trend in solo instrumental jazz. Delmark issued additional albums by Jarman, Abrams, and AACM member Kalaparusha McIntyre. In 1972, Delmark also issued a live album by the Art Ensemble of Chicago.

Iglauer fondly recalled the Delmark/Jazz Record Mart days in the early 1970s as "fast and furious," with operations running "on a cash economy." In the studio with the blues acts, Koester was a "four hours and a bucket of beer session kind of guy," Iglauer said, but he gave musicians much-welcomed latitude. On Friday nights, Koester set up his movie projector for his employees, customers, and friends. "It could get pretty hilarious," Iglauer said. "Bob might take the old 78-rpms he couldn't stand, like something by Kay Kyser, and break the records over people's heads. We would go into clubs, and Bob would get into other people's arguments. Bob was a wild man in those days. Just great times." But Delmark recording activity was slowing to a trickle. Koester had opened a second record store in northern Chicago and also purchased a building. Tight for cash, Koester halted new sessions and allowed some Delmark classics, such as Wells' "Hoodoo Man Blues," to go out of print for several years.

As the 1970s progressed, Iglauer emerged as Chicago's blues impresario with Alligator Records. While with Koester in the early 1970s, Iglauer proposed a recording date for blues singer Hound Dog Taylor and his band, the HouseRockers. When Koester declined, Iglauer financed a session and formed his own label. "The best thing Bob ever did was to take me to a Mexican restaurant and level with me," Iglauer recalled. "He said that since I was spending work hours at Delmark promoting my business, I should go out on my own." After recording just a handful of albums over several years, Iglauer issued records in the late 1970s by Chicago blues performers Albert Collins and singer Koko Taylor which put Alligator on the international stage. Since the 1980s, Alligator has been arguably America's leading blues label. "In a sense, the child outgrew the father," said Iglauer, regarding the relationship between Alligator and Delmark.

By the 1980s, Koester's financial liquidity had improved. He had sold the second store in northern Chicago, and had built up his following at the expanded West Grand Avenue store. Its rising stature among Chicago jazz and blues record buyers and tourists paralleled the neighborhood's growing upscale status. "The whole area around Grand Avenue took off, first with the gays and the yuppies following right behind them," Koester said. "The store prospered right along with it." Finally in 1995, Koester moved the Jazz Record Mart to a larger building on Wabash Avenue.

With the store on firm footing, Koester reactivated Delmark. The label's rise in the 1990s is attributable to new jazz and blues acts, to clever repackaging of old Delmark classics from the vaults (such as Delmark's 40th anniversary blues and jazz compilations), and to Koester's purchase of superb jazz and blues masters from long-defunct labels such as Apollo.

Delmark again provides exposure to superb, lesser-known jazz musicians, largely based in Chicago, such as horn players Malachi Thompson, Rich Corpolongo, and Zane Massey, pianist Jodie Christian, and bassist Willie Kent. *Downbeat* magazine's Critics Poll in 1995 named Delmark "Jazz Label of the Year." In the blues field, Delmark captures the feel of the neighborhood club with releases by Syl Johnson, Jimmy Dawkins, Jimmy Burns, and others. With the Apollo masters, Koester has reissued blues and jazz classics by such artists as Dinah Washington, Coleman Hawkins, Earl Hines, Pete Johnson, and Johnny Hodges. About half of Delmark's revenues are now derived through export sales in such countries as Japan, France, Holland, Greece, Spain, and Italy.

In some ways, the 1990s have been a period of vindication for Koester. Not only has he survived as owner of an independent record

Little Labels—Big Sound

label, but Delmark projects from previous decades are gaining more critical attention than ever before. Nessa teamed up with Koester to remaster onto CD several of Delmark's AACM classics, such as Mitchell's "Sound." Its reissue in 1996, some 30 years after its original release during the turbulent 1960s, attracted headlines in the music press and in the *New York Times*. Again, time was on the side of a courageous Delmark project. "I'm like a lot of guys who simply love the music and want to make a contribution," Koester said. "Sometimes you put wonderful records out there, such as 'Hoodoo Man Blues,' but the world isn't ready for them just yet. It can take years for people to figure out what's going on. You have to learn patience, and it pays off."

173

Delmark Records

LITTLE LABELS ON REISSUE ANTHOLOGIES

Each of the 10 labels profiled are well-represented on vinyl album and CD reissue anthologies. In recent years, surviving owners of these labels have played a vital role in preserving the legacy. Reissues attract a small, loyal audience and go in and out of print, so availability can be unpredictable.

Many companies sell reissue anthologies by mail. They include Ace Records, P.O. Box 9341, Jackson, MS 39206; Rhino Records, 2225 Colorado Ave., Santa Monica, CA 90404; Ace Records (an English company), 46–50 Steele Rd., London, NW10 7AS England; and the clearinghouse Collectors' Choice Music, P.O. Box 838, Itasca, IL 60143-0838 (gordona@ccmusic.com). The following is a sample, but certainly not a comprehensive listing, of interesting CD reissues available.

Gennett Records

Louis Armstrong and King Oliver—Milestone. Contains all 13 Gennett sides by King Oliver's Creole Jazz Band from 1923, including Armstrong's first recorded cornet solos on "Chimes Blues" and "Froggie Moore." Also includes Gennett sides from the Armstrong-led Red Onion Jazz Babies.

Jelly Roll Morton—Milestone. Includes his 16 piano solos for Gennett during 1923–24, among the most significant piano recording sessions in jazz history. Digital remastering couldn't overcome the poor fidelity of the original 78-rpm discs.

Bix Beiderbecke and the Chicago Cornets—Milestone. Marvelous collection of Gennett material, containing the 15 sides by the Wolverine Orchestra from 1924. Also includes sides by Beiderbecke and the Sioux City Six and by Bix and His Rhythm Jugglers.

Paramount Records

Charley Patton: Founder of the Mississippi Blues — Yazoo. One of many excellent Paramount country blues collections from Yazoo Records of Newton, N.J. Yazoo also issued *King of the Delta Blues: The Music of Charlie Patton*. In 1990, Document Records of Vienna, Austria, compiled a four-CD set of Patton's complete recordings in chronological order.

Masters of the Delta Blues: The Friends of Charlie Patton — Yazoo. Compilation of Patton associates Tommy Johnson, Bertha Lee, Son House, and Ishmon Bracey. From exceedingly rare Paramount 78-rpm discs from the late 1920s and early 1930s.

Blind Lemon Jefferson — Milestone and Document. Several reissue anthologies of Jefferson's brilliant Paramount sides are in print. The Milestone collection includes informative notes.

Ma Rainey — Milestone. This 24-song collection finds Rainey backed with some of the era's best jazz musicians. Rainey's Paramount sides appear on numerous Yazoo collections, as well as on Document.

Dial Records

Charlie Parker, The Complete Dial Sessions — Stash. With assistance from former Dial owner Ross Russell, English jazz historian Tony Williams spent years compiling Parker's Dial recordings, including the unissued alternate takes. The four-CD collection contains 89 sides from 1946–47, with up to four takes of some songs. Because Parker never played a song the same way twice, this package is both instructive and spellbinding. Includes "Lover Man," recorded hours before Parker suffered an emotional collapse. First issued on Williams' Spotlite label series in the 1970s.

Dexter Gordon, The Complete Dial Sessions — Stash. A young Gordon

Little Labels on Reissue Anthologies

from 1947, including classic saxophone duels with Wardell Gray and Teddy Edwards.

King Records

Battle of the Blues: Eddie "Cleanhead" Vinson, Roy Brown, Wynonie Harris—King. These blues shouters rock it out on this reissue of an original album rarely seen these days.

The King Box Set—King. This 85-song collection includes 54 charted hits on King and its subsidiary labels. The package contains Bullmoose Jackson's "I Love You, Yes I Do," The Charms' "Hearts of Stone," and Bill Doggett's "Honky Tonk (Part 2)." Includes a 36-page booklet. Available from Collectors' Choice.

James Brown: Star Time—Polydor. His best work throughout his career, beginning with his classic recordings first issued by King and its subsidiary Federal label from 1956–64. Includes a 64-page booklet.

The Five Royales Anthology—Rhino. Two CDs from one of the top 1950s groups. One of many Rhino reissue packages of original King classics.

Duke and Peacock Records

Johnny Ace Memorial Album—MCA. A hits compilation first issued shortly after his death. It stayed in print for years, even after MCA obtained control of Duke's masters. Today, it continues to delight a new generation of fans.

Clarence Gatemouth Brown: The Original Peacock Recordings—Rounder. Twelve songs including "Okie Dokie Stomp," "Sad Hour," and "Just Before Dawn." Captures Gatemouth in his early days with Peacock.

Hound Dog: The Peacock Recordings—MCA. Big Mama Thornton sings "Hound Dog," "Yes, Baby" (a duet with Duke's Johnny Ace), and "Walking Blues."

Bobby Bland, the Duke Recordings—MCA. Three volumes. These cuts

177

by Bland, during his long Duke career, include such lesser-known songs as "Lover with a Reputation," "Playgirl," and "Shoes."

Treat Her Right: The Best of Roy Head—Varese Sarabande. The soulful white Texan with his early soul-rock songs. The singles include "Apple of My Eye," recorded with his band, The Traits. Other cuts come from early Scepter Records tracks produced by Huey Meaux.

Sun Records

Blue Flames: A Sun Blues Collection—Rhino. Features Sam Phillips' early blues recordings by Howlin' Wolf, B. B. King, James Cotton, and others.

Sun Records Harmonica Classics—Rounder. Cuts by Joe Hill Louis, Big Walter Horton, and others.

The Classic Carl Perkins—Bear Family. Five-CD package, with a 24-page booklet. In addition to his Sun recordings, package includes Perkins on Columbia and Decca.

The Sun Sessions CD—*Elvis Presley*—RCA. His entire Sun output from July 1954 to July 1955, including unissued alternate takes. Remarkable collection of country, blues, pop, R&B, and rockabilly songs by a young Presley shortly before his world changed.

Riverside Records

Thanks to the work of former Riverside owner Orrin Keepnews, the label's classic albums are available on CD through Fantasy's Original Jazz Classics series, including comprehensive box set collections. Among the many Riverside albums on CD:

Cannonball Adderly Quintet in San Francisco—Recorded in 1959, it became a Riverside best-seller.

Monk's Music and *Brilliant Corners*—Two of Thelonius Monk's best

Little Labels on Reissue Anthologies

albums, Keepnews showcased the pianist with the era's best players, such as saxophonist John Coltrane.

Wes Montgomery Trio and *Boss Guitar*—Albums issued in 1959 and 1963 respectively, these albums capture the guitar legend in a small group setting.

Everybody Digs Bill Evans—Everybody did after this 1958 Riverside album, reissued by JVC on Extended Resolution CD with excellent clarity.

Ace Records

The Best of Ace—Scotti Brothers. In three volumes, the Ace story is told with affection. Of particular interest is Volume 2's R&B collection, including Earl King's "Those Lonely, Lonely Nights" and Huey "Piano" Smith's "Rockin' Pneumonia and the Boogie Woogie Flu."

Crescent City Soul: The Sound of New Orleans—EMI. Four CDs, 113 songs, including Ace's "Don't You Just Know It" by Huey Smith and the Clowns. Also includes Guitar Slim's "The Things That I Used to Do," produced for Specialty Records by future Ace founder Johnny Vincent.

The Very Best of Jimmy Clanton—Ace (Jackson, Miss.). The Mississippi pop singer's biggest hits on Ace, including "Just a Dream," "Go, Jimmy, Go," and "Venus in Blue Jeans."

Monument Records

The Monument Story—Sony. A double CD compilation of Monument singles. The tapes were remastered with the care associated with label founder Fred Foster. Includes a brief label history by Foster.

Lonely and Blue—Monument/Legacy/Sony. Roy Orbison's lesser-known Monument sides, including "Raindrops" and "Blue Avenue," are packaged with his classics on this fancy 24-karat gold disc with special insert.

The Legendary Roy Orbison—CBS. Four-CD offering includes a 36-page booklet. Includes early Sun releases ("Rock House"), his Monument material, and later MGM recordings. An attractive package, graphically and sonically.

Delmark Records

Junior Wells: Hoodoo Man Blues—Of the more than 100 Delmark albums since the 1950s (with most still in print), this 1965 classic might be the label's crowning achievement. Among the first contemporary Chicago blues albums ever recorded and universally regarded as one of the genre's greatest. Delmark releases can be ordered by mail through the Chicago Record Mart, 444 North Wabash, Chicago, Ill., 60611–3538 or call 800-684-3480.

Delmark 40th Anniversary Blues—Excellent CD sampling of Chicago blues with Junior Wells, Magic Sam, Otis Rush, Jimmy Johnson, and sides by country blues legends Sleepy John Estes and Big Joe Williams.

Delmark 40th Anniversary Jazz—Captures the wide variety of jazz produced by label owner Bob Koester, including influential 1960s free jazz from Roscoe Mitchell and Joseph Jarman.

Roscoe Mitchell: Sound—The 1966 debut album by the Chicago's Association for the Advancement of Creative Musicians grows in stature each year. Mitchell's band includes trumpeter Lester Bowie.

Magic Sam Live—Captures the legendary blues guitarist from a sizzling performance at the 1969 Ann Arbor, Michigan, Blues Festival. Shortly after, Magic Sam died at age 32. Some prefer Magic Sam's only studio album on Delmark, *West Side Soul*.

Little Labels on Reissue Anthologies

NOTES

One / Gennett Records

1. Larry Gara, *The Baby Dodds Story* (Los Angeles: Contemporary Press, 1959), p. 69.
2. Richard Gennett, personal interview with Rick Kennedy, 1991.
3. Hoagland Carmichael, *Sometimes I Wonder* (New York: Farrar, Straus, and Giroux, 1965), p. 140.
4. Interview with Harold Soule, 1964, John MacKenzie Collection, Indiana Historical Society Library, Indianapolis, Ind.
5. Carmichael, *Sometimes I Wonder*, p. 188.
6. Bud Dant, personal interview with Rick Kennedy, 1992.
7. Interview with Joe Geier, 1970, John MacKenzie Collection, Indiana Historical Society Library, Indianapolis, Ind.
8. Interview with Clayton Jackson, 1970, John MacKenzie Collection, Indiana Historical Society Library, Indianapolis, Ind.
9. Ryland Jones, personal interview with Rick Kennedy, 1992.
10. Fred Gennett, personal interview with Rick Kennedy, 1994.

Two / Paramount Records

1. Gayle Dean Wardlow, "The Talent Scouts: H. C. Speir (1895–1972)," *78 Quarterly*, Vol. 1, No. 8 (1994), p. 15.
2. Interview with Mayo Williams, 1970, John MacKenzie Collection, Indiana Historical Society Library, Indianapolis, Ind.
3. Stephen Calt, "The Anatomy of a Race Label Part II," *78 Quarterly*, Vol. 1, No. 4 (1975), p. 17.
4. *The Paramount Book of Blues*, published for The New York

Recording Laboratories, Port Washington, Wisconsin, 1928. (Made available by 78 *Quarterly.*)

5. Ibid.

6. Ibid.

7. Calt, "The Anatomy of a Race Label Part II," p. 20.

8. John Steiner, personal interview with Rick Kennedy, 1995.

9. Gayle Dean Wardlow, personal interview with Rick Kennedy, 1996.

10. Steiner, personal interview with Rick Kennedy, 1995.

Three / Dial Records

1. Ross Russell, personal correspondence with Rick Kennedy, 1995.

2. Ibid.

3. Ibid.

4. *The Bebop Revolution*, edited by David Oliphant (Austin: Harry Ransom Humanities Research Center, University of Texas, 1994), p. 18.

5. Russell correspondence.

6. Ross Russell presentation to the International Association of Jazz Record Collectors, London, England, July 1994.

7. Russell correspondence.

8. Miles Davis with Quincy Troupe, *Miles: The Autobiography* (New York: Simon & Schuster, 1989), p. 85.

9. Russell correspondence.

10. Davis, *Miles: The Autobiography*, p. 89.

11. Ibid., p. 88.

12. *The Bebop Revolution*, p. 24.

13. Russell correspondence.

14. Ibid.

15. Ibid.

Four / King Reocrds

1. James Brown with Bruce Tucker, *James Brown: The Godfather of Soul* (New York: Macmillan, 1986), p. 78.

2. Jim Wilson, personal interview with Randy McNutt, 1990.

3. Jack Ramey, "Jukebox Operator," *The Cincinnati Enquirer*, February 6, 1949.

4. An early 1950s interview with Sydney Nathan. From a story titled

"The Influx of Independents," of unknown publication. Provided by Zella Nathan.

5. Grandpa Jones, personal interview with Randy McNutt, 1991.

6. Arnold Shaw, *Honkers and Shouters* (New York: Collier, 1978), p. 278.

7. Steven C. Tracy, *Going to Cincinnati: A History of Blues in the Queen City* (Chicago: University of Illinois Press, 1993), p. 54. Tracy obtained Glover's quotation from Jon Fox's radio documentary, "King of the Queen City."

8. Ray Pennington, personal interview with Randy McNutt, 1987.

9. Jimmie Logsdon, personal interview with Randy McNutt, 1994.

10. Hal Neely, personal interview with Randy McNutt, 1994.

11. Ray Pennington, personal interview with Randy McNutt, 1987.

12. Hal Neely, personal interview with Randy McNutt, 1994.

13. Robert Santelli, personal interview with Rick Kennedy, 1996.

Five / Duke-Peacock Records

1. Jim Dawson and Steve Propes, *What Was the First Rock 'n' Roll Record* (Boston: Faber and Faber, 1992), p. 116.

2. Alan Govenar, *The Early Years of Rhythm and Blues* (Houston: Rice University Press, 1990), p. 5.

3. Charles White, *The Life and Times of Little Richard, the Quasar of Rock* (New York: Harmony Books, 1984), pp. 37–38.

4. Alan Govenar, *Meeting the Blues: The Rise of the Texas Sound* (Dallas: Taylor Publishing Company, 1988), p. 106.

5. William Holford, personal interview with Randy McNutt, 1995.

6. Larry Willoughby, *Texas Rhythm, Texas Rhyme: A Pictorial History of Texas Music* (Austin: Tonkawa Free Press, 1984), p. 75.

7. *Record World*. April 1973. Week of publication unknown.

8. Ibid.

9. Galen Gart and Roy C. Ames, *Duke/Peacock Records: An Illustrated History with Discography* (Milford, N.H.: Big Nickel Publications, 1990), p. 74.

10. James Mattis, personal interview with Randy McNutt, 1995.

11. "From Memphis to Malaco, Bobby 'Blue' Bland Turns on Your Lovelight!" Mike Streissguth, *Goldmine*, July 21, 1995.

12. Liner notes from *The Soul of the Man, Bobby Bland*, Duke Records LP 79, by Robert J. Sye. Circa 1966.

13. Roy Head, personal interview with Randy McNutt, 1995.

14. Ibid.

15. Galen Gart and Roy C. Ames, *Duke/Peacock Records: An Illustrated History with Discography*, p. 5.

16. Roy Head, personal interview with Randy McNutt, 1995.

Six / Sun Records

1. Colin Escott, with Martin Hawkins, *Good Rockin' Tonight: Sun Records and the Birth of Rock 'n' Roll* (New York: St. Martin's Press, 1991), p. 32.

2. David Halberstam, *The Fifties* (New York: Fawcett Columbine, 1993), p. 470.

3. Malcolm Yelvington, personal interview with Randy McNutt, September 14, 1985.

4. Elton Whisenhunt, "Sam Phillips Recalls How It All Developed," *Billboard*, August 27, 1977.

5. Robert Hilburn, "Cash, after Four Decades, Alone at Last," *Los Angeles Times*, April 29, 1994.

6. Charlie Feathers, personal interview with Randy McNutt, 1986.

7. Carl Perkins, personal interview with Randy McNutt, 1993.

8. Marcus Van Story, personal interview with Randy McNutt, 1986.

9. Joe Edwards, "Billy Lee Riley Reaching for Rock Star Status," *The Cincinnati Enquirer*, January 13, 1984.

10. Roland Janes, personal interview with Randy McNutt, 1986.

11. Robert Kerr, "Blast from the Past," *The Memphis Commercial Appeal*, September 20, 1992.

12. Bill Lee Riley, personal interview with Randy McNutt, 1985.

13. Albert Burgess, personal interview with Randy McNutt, 1985.

14. Barbara Pittman, personal interview with Randy McNutt, 1985.

15. Michael Norman, "Legend Lends Rock Hall Sun Equipment," *Cleveland Plain Dealer*, June 3, 1995.

Seven / Riverside Records

1. Orrin Keepnews, interview with Rick Kennedy, 1994. All other quotes from Keepnews in this chapter, unless otherwise indicated, were derived from this interview.

2. Ibid.

3. Keepnews, *The View from Within (Jazz Writings, 1948–87)* (New York: Oxford University Press, 1988), p. 121.

4. Pat Metheny, interview with Rick Kennedy, 1983.

184

5. Keepnews, *The View from Within*, p. 174.
6. Ibid., p. 204.
7. Ralph Gleason liner notes for the Prestige album, *Piano Giants, Vol. I*, 1975.

Eight / Ace Records

1. John Vincent, interviews with Randy McNutt, 1995. All other quotes from Vincent in this chapter were derived from these interviews, unless noted.
2. Personal interview with Cosimo Matassa, 1995.
3. Dr. John (Mac Rebennack), *Under a Hoodoo Moon: The Life of the Night Tripper* (New York: St. Martin's Griffin, 1994), p. 74.
4. Frankie Ford, interview with Randy McNutt, 1980.
5. Ibid.
6. "Breaking Ground, Ace-Vee-Jay Deal Called Biggest Ever of Its Kind," *Billboard*, 1962 (exact date unknown).

Nine / Monument Records

1. Fred Foster, personal interview with Randy McNutt, 1994. All subsequent quotes are derived from the same interview except where noted.
2. Boudeleaux Bryant, "The Personal Side of Fred Foster," *Billboard*, December 21, 1968.
3. Boudeleaux Bryant, liner notes, *Orbisongs*.
4. Monument advertisement in *Billboard*, 1977. Date unknown.
5. Grandpa Jones, personal interview with Randy McNutt, 1991.
6. Wayne Moss, personal interview with Randy McNutt, 1994.

Ten / Delmark Records

1. Bruce Iglauer, interviews with Rick Kennedy, 1996. All other quotes from Iglauer in this chapter were derived from these interviews.
2. Robert Koester, interviews with Rick Kennedy, 1996. All other quotes from Koester in this chapter were derived from these interviews.
3. Chuck Nessa, interview with Rick Kennedy, 1996.
4. Frank Powers, interview with Rick Kennedy, 1996.
5. Bill Dahl, *The Blues: The Expert's Guide to the Best Blues Recordings* (San Francisco: Miller Freeman Books, 1966), p. 134.

SELECTED BIBLIOGRAPHY

Britt, Stan. *Long Tall Dexter.* London: Quartet Books, 1989.

Broven, John. *Rhythm and Blues in New Orleans.* Gretna, La.: Pelican Books, 1974.

Brown, James, and Bruce Tucker. *James Brown: The Godfather of Soul.* New York: Macmillan, 1986.

Calt, Stephen, and Gayle Wardlow. *King of the Delta Blues: The Life and Music of Charlie Patton.* Newton, N.J.: Rock Chapel Press, 1988.

Cantor, Louis. *Wheelin' on Beale.* New York: Pharos Books, 1992.

Carmichael, Hoagland. *Sometimes I Wonder.* New York: Farrar, Straus, and Giroux, 1965.

Carmichael, Hoagland. *The Stardust Road* (1946). Reissue, Bloomington: Indiana University Press, 1983.

Clayson, Alan. *Only the Lonely: Roy Orbison's Life and Legacy.* New York: St. Martin's Press, 1989.

Davis, Miles, with Quincy Troupe. *Miles: The Autobiography.* New York: Simon & Schuster, 1989.

Dawson, Jim, and Steve Propes. *What Was the First Rock 'n' Roll Record?* Boston: Faber and Faber, 1992.

Dixon, R. M. W., and J. Godrich. *Recording the Blues.* London: Hatch, 1970.

Escott, Colin, and Martin Hawkins. *Good Rockin' Tonight: Sun Records and the Birth of Rock 'n' Roll.* New York: St. Martin's Press, 1991.

Gart, Galen, and Roy C. Ames. *Duke/Peacock Records: An Illustrated History with Discography.* Milford, N.H.: Big Nickel Publications, 1990.

Gillett, Charlie. *The Sound of the City: The Rise of Rock and Roll.* New York: Pantheon Books, 1983.

Govenar, Alan. *Meeting the Blues: The Rise of the Texas Sound.* Dallas: Taylor Publishing Co., 1988.

Hardy, Phil, and David Laing. *The Faber Companion to 20th Century Popular Music.* London: Faber and Faber Ltd., 1990.

Harrison, Max, Charles Fox, and Eric Hacker. *The Essential Jazz Records, Ragtime to Swing*. London: Mansell Publishing, 1984.

John, Dr. (Mac Rebennack), with Jack Rummel. *Under a Hoodoo Moon: The Life of the Night Tripper*. New York: St. Martin's Griffin, 1994.

Jones, Louis M. "Grandpa," and Charles K. Wolfe. *Everybody's Grandpa*. Knoxville: The University of Tennessee Press, 1984.

Keepnews, Orrin. *The View from Within (Jazz Writings, 1948–87)*. Oxford: Oxford University Press, 1988.

Kennedy, Rick. *Jelly Roll, Bix, and Hoagy: Gennett Studios and the Birth of Recorded Jazz*. Bloomington: Indiana University Press, 1994.

Malone, Bill C. *Country Music U.S.A.* Austin: University of Texas Press, 1985.

McNutt, Randy. *We Wanna Boogie: An Illustrated History of the American Rockabilly Movement*. Hamilton, Ohio: The Hamilton Hobby Press, Inc., 1988.

Oliphant, Dave, ed. *The Bebop Revolution in Words and Music*. Austin: Harry Ransom Humanities Research Center, The University of Texas at Austin, 1994.

Oliver, Paul, Max Harrison and William Bolcom. *The New Grove Gospel, Blues & Jazz*. New York: W.W. Norton & Co., 1986.

Palmer, Robert. *Deep Blues*. New York: Viking Penguin, 1981.

Parton, Dolly. *Dolly: My Life and Other Unfinished Business*. New York: Harper-Collins, 1994.

Russell, Russ. *Bird Lives! The High Life and Hard Times of Charlie 'Yardbird' Parker*. London: Quartet Books, 1973.

Rust, Brian. *American Record Label Book*. New Rochelle, N.Y.: Arlington House, 1978.

Santelli, Robert. *The Big Book of Blues, A Biographical Encyclopedia*. New York: Penguin Books, 1993.

Tracy, Steven C. *Going to Cincinnati: A History of the Blues in the Queen City*. Chicago: The University of Illinois Press, 1993.

Ward, Ed, Geoffrey Stokes, and Ken Tucker. *Rock of Ages: The Rolling Stone History of Rock & Roll*. New York: Rolling Stone Press/Summit Books, 1986.

Whitburn, Joel. *Top Pop, 1955–1982*. Menomonee Falls, Wis.: Record Research, Inc., 1983.

Whitburn, Joel. *Top R&B Singles, 1942–1988*. Menomonee Falls, Wis.: Record Research, Inc., 1988.

White, Charles. *The Life and Times of Little Richard, the Quasar of Rock*. New York: Harmony Books, 1984.

Willoughby, Larry. *Texas Rhythm, Texas Rhyme: A Pictorial History of Texas Music*. Austin: Tonkawa Free Press, 1984.

Selected Bibliography

INDEX

193

Index

194

Index

Rick Kennedy, a media relations manager with General Electric, worked for a decade as a journalist. Kennedy plays jazz piano and is the author of *Jelly Roll, Bix, and Hoagy: Gennett Studios and the Birth of Recorded Jazz* (Indiana University Press).

Randy McNutt is a longtime reporter with the *Cincinnati Enquirer* and the author of *We Wanna Boogie: An Illustrated History of the American Rockabilly Movement* and a book on Ohio ghost towns.